Basic Bible Storying

Preparing and Presenting Bible Stories for Evangelism, Discipleship, Training, and Ministry

Revised Edition

J. O. Terry

Church Starting Network

Basic Bible Storying

Preparing and Presenting Bible Stories for Evangelism, Discipleship, Training, and Ministry

Requests for information should be addressed to:

Church Starting Network
3515 Sycamore School Rd. # 125-161
Fort Worth, Texas 76133

www.churchstarting.net

smith_ebbie@yahoo.com

Library of Congress Cataloging-in-Publication Data

J.O. Terry

Basic Bible Storying

ISBN 0-9772433-4-6

Cover design by: Moonlight-Studios, Daniel E. Sanchez

Printed and bound in the United States of America

Dedicated to the Goals: That we, in our lifetimes, might:

- *Recover the skill and joy of telling the Bible stories so that all who have never heard might hear and be saved,*
- *Observe oral learners, whether their orality stems from their lack of reading ability or from their own preferences, to find ways to present the Bible stories for their understanding, salvation, and growth in their knowledge of Christ as Savior,*
- *Rejoice as these oral learners keep God's Word alive in their memory and retelling to spread the Gospel among their own peoples to the end that New Testament churches continue growing among their people,*
- *Seek those who have resisted traditional Bible teaching and preaching but who are open to stories that can soften their hardened hearts,*
- *Minister to those in need of spiritual encouragement of God's love and provision in their life circumstances,*
- *And accept the blessings of seeing God glorified through the continued telling of the stories from His Story.*

Contents

Foreword

Welcome to the world of Bible Storying. Since the rediscovery of Bible Storying as an effective and viable method for presenting the gospel, discipling believers, and training emerging church leaders, there have been many requests for Bible Storying materials and training. This manual grows out of those requests, out of my own personal experience during Bible Storying in many Asian countries, and out of my opportunities in training beginning Bible storyers among our missionaries, church workers, and national coworkers.

Two tensions inform the effort:

- *To keep the manual uncomplicated so that anyone can read it and get a practical working knowledge of Bible Storying, and*
- *To keep the manual comprehensive enough so that after one has studied it, there are relatively few questions left unanswered.*

While much of the present methodology has come from actual practice in Bible Storying and training storyers while a missionary in Asia, it is really not a new methodology. The Bible itself has many examples of the use of storying to teach, warn, and encourage. I will say more on this in the following Introduction. In addition, numerous historical references point to a continued use of Bible stories in narrated and dramatized form over the centuries. It is beyond the purpose of this text to enumerate these accounts.

The preparation for Bible Storying is an objectively tailored edition of curriculum development which requires basically knowing both the message to be taught (extent and organization) and the characteristics which include learning preferences and abilities of the intended audience. The practice of actual Bible Storying or Bible story-driven teaching is a compilation of good andragogical practice which would be at home in any classroom, especially among those who are preliterate or who needed or preferred an oral-based learning methodology. The concept has been modified to suit the specialized needs of Bible Storying, married to the strategies related to support of a Church Planting Movement, and related to the various crises and need ministries common to missionaries and church workers in the U.S. A. and in other countries.

The beginning Bible storyer may be tempted to take one of the existing popular model sets of Bible Storying lessons, translate the story lessons verbatim, and begin using them. While this may serve to produce some quick, though limited results, it must be realized that each story lesson model must be crafted for addressing worldview issues in culturally acceptable ways and means to the end that biblical truths speak clearly to a particular group of listeners. If the new listener group happens to be similar in worldview and at about the same point in their spiritual knowledge and quest as a group for whom the Bible story lessons were originally crafted, the use of existing models may produce acceptable results. As the worldview differences between the original and new listener groups increase, the end results typically become more unpredictable.

As the worldview that the existing Bible Storying model is based on differs from the worldview of the new listener group, unanswered questions may arise and many spiritual issues can remain unchallenged and unaddressed. The greatest danger comes when too much is assumed, leaving the new listener group without adequate scriptural background to understand their accountability to God for their sins, their helplessness to provide the needed atonement for sin, the fact that only God can forgive sin through his provision, and the reality of a relationship to God only through Christ as Savior.

Two problem areas stem from the failure to customize the Bible Storying process for particular peoples and their worldviews. First, the failure to address spiritual issues can and does lead to potential syncretism. Second, failure to customize the storying to the culture may increase the resistance and hostility of the listeners by actually inoculating them against the gospel. By the inappropriate choice and crafting of stories or poorly adapted lessons and teaching themes, Bible storyers may delay or obstruct the acceptance of the Message.

For these reasons, the reader is urged to be patient and to carefully follow this manual for storying. This manual leads through a step-by-step development process which should help the beginning Bible storyer to become knowledgeable in adapting existing Bible Storying models to fit his/her group's needs or to develop a new model particularly suited for a new target listener group.

This process is not an exercise in cleverness leading to sure-fire instant results. The Bible storyer is partnering with the Holy Spirit to teach the listeners through God's Word leading to salvation and beginning a discipled life as a believer. It is the work of the Holy Spirit to bring understanding of the communicated Word and conviction of sin leading to salvation through knowing Christ as Savior and Lord. The Bible storyer is the messenger who relates to the listeners and leads them to hear and consider the implication for their lives.

So the beginning Bible storyer should take the time to develop a storying model that is sensitive to the worldview issues of the listener group's culture. In this case, the model can be shared with colleagues as a written model, or taught as an oral model, to both literate and non-literate leaders, equipping many to share in the continued Bible teaching.

While the primary purposes of most Bible Storying models are that of evangelizing and planting a church, the method has merit and effectiveness for discipling existing believers, training emerging church leaders, and ministering to all listeners in need of encouragement and comfort during times of crises in their individual lives and community. In addition, the method supports both a growth in knowledge of God's Word and its message of salvation and discipleship, and also competence in the practice of teaching the Word to others so they may benefit and in turn become competent.

The Bible storyer will receive many blessings from involvement in this type of proclamation ministry. The new Bible storyer will experience a renewed appreciation for the richness of God's Word in speaking to all cultures and peoples. He/she will also find a personal blessing arising from his/her own deeper understanding of the Bible's story of God and mankind.

It must not be assumed that Bible Storying is only for non-literates and other oral learners. Stories speak to every level of literacy, education, and sophistication. The desire is not to deny anyone an opportunity to know Jesus because of his/her lack of literacy, their oral learning preferences, lack of Scriptures in their spoken language, or simply a lack of understanding that God's Word is relevant whatever their spiritual disposition. Bible Storying is for everyone and can be adapted for teaching all who will listen. This manual guides those who embark on the journey to realize how to do this task.

This writer owes a debt of gratitude to colleagues of the New Tribes Mission (Philippines) for sharing their own concepts of Chronological Bible Teaching that served as my introduction to Bible Storying and to many others among Southern Baptist missionaries in the Philippines. I also owe a debt of gratitude to James B. (Jim) Slack for his early encouragement and invitations to join him in teaching and sharing in the development of the Bible Storying methodology in wide use today. And I must mention my first Bible teaching mentor, Johani (Boy) Gauran of the Philippines for patiently leading me through the basic understanding of the Chronological Bible Teaching approach. At the time Johani was already an experienced Bible story trainer for the Tribal Evangelism, Agriculture, and Community Health (TEACH) training for out-of-school Filipino youths. My joy stems from having many opportunities to make use of the Bible Storying methodology and strategies while learning to use them.

This text is based largely on the writer's own personal experience from the time of first being made aware of the possibilities of Chronological Bible Teaching methodology then being used in the Philippines, through the first personal attempts to teach and then begin personally using the chronological teaching methodology in several South Asian countries. Many of the concepts shared were first rooted in overcoming early mistakes and poor results among peoples different from those living in the Philippines. Later after gaining a level of experience in actual use it was then possible to systematize what was apparently working and to test it out to see if the same concepts worked in other places. The original focus was on primarily Chronological Bible Teaching and later Chronological Bible Storying as a major strategy and methodology. In time, growing experience and new situations pointed toward the need to broaden the basic concepts of using Bible stories in new and creative ways to take advantage of emerging new opportunities. After retiring from missionary field service in 2003, this writer is indebted to many active Bible storyers who have so generously shared from their own experiences and even problems and mistakes so that as a trainer I might continue learning and staying on the cutting edge of Bible Storying. I rejoice that other books and publications in support of the development and use of Bible Storying are now appearing. These new publications reflect the experience and planning of many individuals, teams and agencies who are partnering in making God's Word widely accessible in this generation and reproducible among the world's oral communicators.

J. O. Terry, the developer of this Manual, served as Media Consultant among twenty-four Asia-Pacific and South Asian countries for over three decades and an additional two years consulting on oral Bible strategies in Central America. Specific experience in Bible Storying began in early 1988 which led to development of much of the methodology in use today for preparing Bible story sets for many different people groups. He currently teaches Bible Storying on invitation from churches and mission associations, schools of church planting, and during seminary intensive Chronological Bible Storying classes. He is currently an active participant in the International Orality Network (ION).

Chapter 1

Introduction to Bible Storying

Bible Storying, as a missionary method of proclamation, has been in use since biblical times. In recent years, this method has come into increased and extensive use in evangelistic and church-development efforts around the world. While Bible Storying was first and most extensively used in two Third World areas, the method is coming into expanded use in the West as well. Bible Storying is proving to be an effective method for evangelism, church starting, Christian growth, leadership training, and personal ministry. We embark, therefore, on an exciting and important study.

The Biblical Mention of Storying

In the Scriptures, one finds mention of storying as a method of communication and proclamation. We can follow with confidence this means of telling the Good News of Jesus and God's Salvation.

The writer of Mark's Gospel says,

> On another occasion Jesus began to teach by the lake.... (Mk. 4:1) He taught them many things by parables.... (Mk. 4:2). He did not say anything to them without using a parable (Mk. 4:34).

The Apostle Paul said on two occasions,

> These things happened to them as examples and were written down as warnings for us... (1 Cor. 10:11). (Referring to stories of Israel.)

> For everything that was written in the past was written to teach us, so that through endurance and encouragement of the Scriptures we might have hope. (Ro. 15:4).

John said in his Gospel,

> Jesus did many other miraculous signs....which are not recorded in this book. But these are written that you may believe that Jesus is the

> Christ, the Son of God, and that by believing you may have life in his name. (Jn. 20:30-31).

The Psalmist admonished,

> O my people, hear my teaching; listen to the words of my mouth. I will open my mouth in parables, I will utter things hidden from of old—things we have heard and known, things our fathers have told us. We will not hide them from their children; we will tell the next generation the praiseworthy deeds of the Lord, his power and the wonders he has done." (Ps. 78:1-4).

Peter added,

> We did not follow cleverly invented stories when we told you about the power and coming of our Lord Jesus Christ. (2Pe. 1:16).

This manual seeks to describe and to explain Bible Storying as a distinct method of proclaiming, teaching, and applying biblical truth in the present world.

Bible Storying—What is It?

We begin with a Storying definition. The dictionary defines *story* as the "Narrating of an event or series of events, either true or fictitious." And *storying* as "To tell as a story."[1] While the word *storying* as a gerund doesn't translate well to other languages, it is descriptive of a primary characteristic of the method. Others use the terms "Bible storytelling" or "biblical storytelling". *Storying* is a common word on the internet and has been popularized in the titles of several books on management and administration as well as many references in education and self-development writings.

Bible Storying is the *intentional* and *uninterrupted sharing* of God's Word primarily as stories. These stories are usually supplemented with culturally appropriate learning exercises that are listener sensitive. The stories may be told as part of a strategy of telling many stories leading to an invitation to believe, or may be only a few stories during an evangelistic encounter or a ministry opportunity.

What is very important to remember is that listeners prefer each story to be continuous and uninterrupted from start to finish. Some chronological Bible teachers have a practice of telling a portion of the story and then stopping the story to comment on some point of interest. Oral learners prefer and respond better to stories that are delivered without inserted comment or pauses to teach which interrupt the narrative.

Two additional practices that often prove less effective with oral learners are teaching from the stories without actually telling the events as a story, and the practice of deeply paraphrasing a story in which teaching comment is inserted as part of the story itself. These concepts will be further elaborated in later sections on crafting stories and telling the stories to listeners.

The other characteristic of Bible Storying being intentional speaks to the fact that Bible stories are told for definite purposes for achieving objectives such as:

- *evangelizing unbelievers,*
- *planting a church among new believers,*
- *discipling new believers,*
- *training emerging church leaders, and*
- *ministering to felt needs during times of crises as a prelude to evangelism.*

The attempt to reach these objectives demands that the stories are not chosen because they are popular, or the favorite of the storyer, but are related to the purpose for telling the stories, and are informed by significant spiritual worldview and cultural characteristics of the listeners. The Bible storyer deliberately and carefully chooses the best stories for each purpose. In addition, stories must provide continuity to the teaching while providing interest and enhancing acceptance by the listeners. More will be said about this in considering the effect of worldview issues on the choice of stories and the Storying Session when Bible stories are told.

While there is need for the storyer to be intentional in choice of Bible stories, it is not uncommon to find that in working with many of the peoples who are oral learners that their choice of stories is intuitive. They choose stories that appeal to them in some manner and that somehow speak to their felt needs. But they may not be able to tell why they choose the stories. Let me illustrate.

For several years I taught Bible stories to rural church leaders and evangelists in Bangladesh. These were five-day training camps during which I taught as many as 75-80 stories chronologically. What I want to point out is that after I had taught through all these stories and associated pictures with the stories, the workers would then choose and come to agreement on stories they felt were best for their people by choosing the pictures associated with each story.

Later I would take their choice of stories and reteach them in chronological order. I had carefully chosen the larger number of stories based on my understanding of the Bengali listeners' worldview and the truths that needed to be taught to evangelize and disciple their people. Perhaps my list of stories was too many to remember, or some of the stories were difficult for someone without my knowledge to feel comfortable in telling.

The workers invariably chose around forty stories and the selection in each location showed a remarkable similarity. Later I requested publishing of a limited set of Bible teaching pictures which accompanied only those most commonly chosen stories. Among the commonly chosen stories were the stories of Adam and Eve, the Flood, Feeding of the Multitude, and the Prodigal Son. Those being trained could not always give a rationale for their choice of stories. But there was some intuitive process that led them to their selections. I realized that my task was to help them get to these stories while being sure their list included stories needed for faith and growth in Christ.

Since many of these men and women were not literate it was essential that I tell as many Bible stories as practical during the training to at least give them access to a larger library of stories. This library of stories allowed them to choose intuitively the ones they would use. There were times when I challenged their choices just to see why they chose that story. The closest I ever got to an answer is "Our people are like that!" I took this to mean that their people had some identification with the particular story.

This larger list of stories in time became part of an Oral Bible the listeners were acquiring. In the initial training sessions most of the listeners had no idea how the stories were linked together and that there was a progression or larger storyline evolving. It was an interesting thing to watch their response as the stories continued and they perceived that the Bible stories were related to one another in a progression or storyline.

Beyond the initial list of stories taught in the training there was need to continue exposing these oral leaders to a wider field of Bible stories. This wider exposure to Bible stories allowed them to grow in their knowledge of the Bible. Also, the greater list of stories included additional stories for sharing with their people as the Holy Spirit directed to disciple, admonish, and correct errors in their faith.

Chapter 2

Rationale for Bible Storying

One of the original purposes for seeking a story-based teaching method was that of providing a culturally and educationally appropriate method for tribal work. Since New Tribes missionaries in the Philippines were already engaged in tribal work, the chronological teaching methodology that was beginning to work for them was appealing for Southern Baptist missionaries as well. At the time as Media Consultant for that region I was concerned about evangelistic methodology that was reproducible, affordable, and culturally appropriate. There were other factors which pointed to the evolving storying methodology as being a good choice.

The Factor of Orality

Orality is the communication and learning characteristic that expresses one's dependence and/or preference upon the spoken word as the basic mode for sharing thoughts, ideas, observations and experiences. These communications are generally shared as stories or other narratively organized forms. In addition, visual cues in the form of gestures, body language and other visual presentations such as flat pictures, models, demonstrations, singing, dancing, and drama are often included in oral communication forms.

Jim Slack, church growth consultant for the International Mission Board, SBC, expressed concern during the late 1980s about the largely non-literate World A that was just beginning to be addressed in a Bold Mission Thrust. Jim was familiar with pioneering work by New Tribes Mission in the Philippines in their use of Chronological Bible Teaching. He saw in this approach an answer to the issue of orality and the barrier that non-literacy had for many traditional evangelistic methods. Jim wrote a paper in which he described the nature of the orality need and of the possibility of teaching in a manner that skirted the literacy barrier for the unreached oral World A.

Orality continues to be a major challenge in the unreached, unevangelized, and undiscipled world. A tension exists between the approach of teaching literacy so the non-literate can read the Bible and witnessing materials, and in temporarily skirting the literacy issue to teach the Bible orally leading to salvation, discipling, and church development. While this would seem to be a simple decision to make—teach non-literates to read and give them the written materials—it is complicated by many factors.

Some African peoples are regressing to orality to save their cultures. Major cultures still do not aggressively provide literacy for women. Among West African Muslims there is a prevailing idea that if the Prophet of Islam was non-literate, so it is a virtue to be non-literate. Those who live in cultures that have survived as oral cultures usually retain their preferred learning mode as oral. So the real issue is not so much literacy vs. oral Bible teaching. The greater question is that of providing better access in this generation for all to hear God's Plan of Redemption and have a reasonable opportunity to respond to it. Discipling, planting a church, and guiding listeners to become persons who can share the Gospel with their own people become the ultimate goals.

The Factor of Oral Learners

The term, *oral learners,* is becoming the preferred term for non-literates, oral communicators, and those preferring to learn orally whether they are functionally literate or not. The term *non-literate* is used here rather than *illiterate.* The term illiterate has been widely used but many consider it pejorative. Other terms, like preliterate and functionally non-literate, characterize persons that are predisposed to be oral learners.

A second circumstance leads to the condition known as Secondary *Orality.* In this category of oral learners, persons generally function as literate though they prefer to learn orally via recorded media or visually through various electronic and film media. The important thing to remember is that if orality is the people's preferred way to learn, the Christian communicator will seek to garner their attention and communicate with them through orality methods. The methods that use orality may be supplemented by print, print-organized messages, and media means that are appropriate and interesting to the people.

The Factor of Reproducibility

Reproducibility remains one of the original concerns of Bible Storying. Indeed, encouraging and allowing reproducibility must be integral in every ongoing missiological task. The goal is to encourage reproducibility.

There are several factors related to local reproducibility:

- *The method must rely on minimal cost and be locally sustainable, not relying on imported teaching materials or equipment.*
- *The method must be culturally appropriate so that the message is at home in the culture.*
- *The method must be educationally simple so that it can be taught and easily learned so as to sustain multi-generations of teaching both by emerging oral learner leaders and by any one of the listeners.*

Bible Storying may be the most reproducible of all missionary methods. Most new converts, even those who cannot read, or who read with difficulty, can learn the basics of storying. This method opens the way to unlimited reproducibility.

The Factor of Overcoming Resistance and Hostility

Resistance & Hostility to the Gospel and its proclamation exist widely. This widespread factor of resistance has sometimes grown out of previous unsuccessful teaching attempts and preaching methodologies that the people consider Western and thereby foreign. Among followers of other religions change or conversion might not come easily. Some listeners may have been inoculated to resist the Christian message.

In addition, open hostility to the presence of a Bible continues in some countries as well as a suspicion regarding its reliability. Some groups tend to reject Christians in general and also to reject things considered Christian including common biblical vocabulary and terminology. Bible stories can avoid some of this resistance and avert much of the hostility if the teaching is carefully chosen, alertly prepared, and sensitively taught from a narrative base.

Event & Group Focus—Many oral learners are attracted to events more so than to new ideas. Because Bible Storying is an event, it is attractive as it fosters community, allowing a group to gather and to participate. Group response reinforces the response of individuals in the group. One characteristic of oral learners is their preference to learn in groups vs. the typically individual learning of literates.

Relational—As a communal event the storyer relates to the listeners. Over time and many sessions trust builds between the storyer and listeners and between listeners and the message. An adequate Bible Storying strategy can provide enough time for this to occur, leading to positive response and closure.

The Factor of Access to Scripture

Many peoples in the world today have limited access to Scripture. Bible Storying can provide this necessary access to Scripture for those lacking Scripture in their mother tongue. Through the stories, proverbs, memory verses, and other passages, people can become aware of biblical teachings whether they are literate or oral learners.

For those who have yet unwritten languages, an Oral Bible communicated through Bible Storying provides access to a "Living Bible" which can be recalled and shared from memory until such time as a proper written Bible translation can be provided and literacy taught. The teachings of Christianity in the early period of the Church relied on the oral transmission of the Gospel.

The Factor of Good Missiology

The goal of a church-planting movement is to set in motion a sustainable evangelism and church planting thrust among a people. Any methodology that supports and encourages this is, therefore, a good choice. If people groups are to be reached with the gospel so the whole group in time is penetrated, it must be done from an ethnocentric perspective from within the group. Bible Storying provides a method that can gain ethnocentric access, be acceptable culturally, and foster continuous reproducibility. Bible Storying fits in with good missionary methodology.

The Factor of Versatility

A viable missionary method must be versatile. One characteristic of Bible Storying is its versatility for use among not only non-literates but also literates of all degrees of reading competency. For this reason, Bible Storying is finding use in the United States and other regions of the Western world as well as on the mission field. There are already many instances of inner city use with immigrants, the Deaf, children's groups, sports teams, divorce recovery groups, coffee-house ministry, hard living and "down and out" folks, and personal life needs.

Beyond the varied inner city uses are needs among Native Americans and Gypsies who are culturally fond of stories. A growing place for use of Bible narratives as stories in preaching, is taking hold especially among younger congregations and those affected by postmodern thinking. The versatility of Bible Storying makes it a viable choice as a missionary and ministry methodology.

Chapter 3

Considering the Listeners

Before considering the process of selecting and preparing Bible stories, it is good to pause to consider the characteristics of one's listeners. In storying practice, a wide range of literacy and orality competencies and preferences among potential listeners comes into play. Knowing these characteristics in advance is extremely helpful in selecting and preparing Bible stories and knowing how the stories should be told to listeners for their best interest and comprehension.

The term Oral Learners has already been introduced as the common way of referring to those who are limited in their literacy or who prefer orality as the way to learn new things. It is not the purpose of this manual to go into a lengthy description or explanation regarding the orality/literacy continuum.

Following are the five typical categories with a brief description of each.

Primary Oral Communicators

Primary Oral Communicators are people who cannot read or write, or, if so, only in the most rudimentary manner. They almost totally depend upon hearing stories and proverbs, gestures, demonstrations, and observation of objects for their learning. In turn, they also communicate in actual stories or virtual stories. In his account of working among non-literates in Indonesia, Hans Rudi Weber says: "In describing a person the illiterate would not talk about the character but rather tell significant stories about him."[2] In another account Johannes Warneck writes,

> "How does the picture of God arise in the mind of the heathen?...through the simple narration of what God has done for men; that these stories are better fitted than any well thought out address for making blinded idolaters acquainted with the living God; the simple telling of what God has done in the course of human history makes his image plastic to them...."[3]

Oral stories are the primary mode of communicating important news and passing heritage information from generation to generation among these peoples.

Functional Non-literates

Functional non-literates are persons who have some reading and writing ability but, due to their limited literacy and education, the persons rely mainly on orality to function in everyday life. The great danger for literate Bible teachers is to assume that because functional non-literates can read some that they can learn well from written materials or from oral materials that are organized in literate propositional manner.

In my experience among functional non-literate rural leaders among the *Kui* in India, the men often had 3-4 years of very low level rural education, did not possess a Bible in their spoken language, and were only marginally literate at best. They were able to read their Bibles with much hesitation and difficulty. An illustration of how Bible Storying helps these functional non-literates comes from Bangladesh.

One of my translators who is highly literate in his own language told me that after hearing the stories told in English he could now read them with greater understanding in his Bengali language. Others among the *Kui* who were only marginally literate demonstrated a greater facility in reading the stories from their Bibles after they had learned the stories orally.

Semiliterates

Semiliterates are defined as those who have a degree of literacy that allows them to function as literates in their society. They are not, however, able to profitably handle lengthy texts and would be very uncomfortable in reading which required analysis or extracting ideas and listing them as organized propositions. Stories have great appeal for these though they can and do read enough to gain access to uncomplicated written materials. Like functional non-literates, they can read something better after they already know what it says. The written words provided cues to a text or knowledge they already possessed.

Among the *Koch* leaders in Bangladesh, I found that many of the pastors and evangelists who came for Bible story training were actually semi-literate in Bengali. Again I heard that comment from a leader: "Now that you have told us the stories, we can read them better in our language and understand them."

Literates

Literates are the people who are average readers and writers. They have acquired enough reading and writing skill to be comfortable using it not only in everyday life but also in acquiring new ideas and expressing them in writing. They will be able to read a Bible of recent translation and gain understanding from it. Depending upon their culture and oral preferences they may still teach biblical truth to others through oral methodologies. One advantage literates enjoy is the ability to write notes, make lists, and to organize ideas and truths categorically. Stories provide entertainment and serve to share memorable events with others.

Highly Literate

Highly literate persons are those who, either through advanced study or their profession, have acquired reading and writing skills well beyond the average. In my own experience I have found that many leaders who are highly literate and have received advanced theological training have great difficulty in communicating to those of lesser literacy. This is compounded when they live in countries where all religious or other literary works are written in a literary high language that is not spoken in everyday conversation, or that their literacy and education is a source of pride that must be demonstrated in their own communication efforts.

The bottom line is that all these categories of orality and literacy can understand stories. Further, their culture may favor stories even when they have the literacy competency to handle more highly organized propositional and expositional materials whether presented in lecture or in writing.

There is not a sharp dividing line between each of these five categories but rather a continuum or gradual merging from one to the other. And many who live in semiliterate cultures may go through a cycle of orality when young, growing literacy during the education years, and a fading of literacy in the adult years. Aging persons, living in an oral society, tend to return to orality in later years due to diminishing eyesight and reversion to their oral culture. In some African societies there are those who function in a literate world when working but revert to an oral world at home or among their extended family in rural areas.

Comparing Characteristics of Oral and Literate Learners

One helpful way to understand the literate storyer's relationship to oral listeners is to compare the characteristics of a typical oral learner with those of a typical literate learner. For more in-depth reading on these characteristics read Walter Ong's text on orality and literacy, especially chapters 3 and 6.[4]

Fig. 1 Oral and Literate Learners Compared

Oral Learners	*Literate Learners*
▪ Knowledge source: nature, kinship, community, elders	▪ Knowledge source: teachers, printed page, multimedia
▪ Enjoys learning in group or community through participation	▪ Prefers learning quietly as individual in isolation
▪ Learns best through stories	▪ Prefers textual summaries, lists, principles
▪ Stores truth in remembered stories & proverbs	▪ Stores truth in written abstracts & principles
▪ Reasons intuitively, experientially	▪ Reasons analytically, logically
▪ Enjoys & comfortable with repetition	▪ Avoids redundancy & repetition
▪ Relational, genealogical	▪ Factual, historical
▪ Holistic (whole is more important than parts)	▪ Segmented (deconstructed parts are of value)
▪ Creative reconstruction of stories and events in sharing	▪ Verbatim memory and written factual accounts for sharing

The comparisons are general observations and should not to be taken as absolute characteristics. Understanding these comparisons, however, should give the literate storyer a better feel for how best to communicate to oral learners. The list is neither in any priority order nor is it exhaustive. Knowing these can be helpful in your storying.

The storyer should also be aware of other characteristics of oral learners. While it has been recorded that some non-literates can hear something once and then recall it verbatim, this is not generally the case in my experience. Repetition definitely fosters a better recall which even then may be a creative reconstruction modified by the listener's own worldview, experience, and social norms.

Oral learners tend to be very practical in what they remember. Since they only know what they can recall, they give highest attention to what is relational and practical, not what is speculative or theoretical. Stories that are closer to their actual lives and that suggest teaching that is do-able or acceptable will gain the greatest attention. So their orality is a limited ability that must be considered when teaching oral learners. Things that are no longer useful or that no longer have immediate value tend to drop off the edge or fade to be replaced by new thoughts that are more useful.

In addition, there is the problem of syncretism where new ideas or teachings are modified by existing local beliefs and experiences. Fading does occur over time so that oral learners typically need to be refreshed by an outside source, by those within their society whose role is to remember heritage events and teachings, by exercising the teaching through recall and retelling, or through playback of recorded teaching. Finally it is generally important to adapt or structure what is communicated or taught to oral learners so that it is in a form and language that is as close to their preferences as possible to limit the amount of restructuring and selective editing they will do in recalling it and sharing with others.

Chapter 4

Basic Bible Storying Tasks

There are a number of basic Bible Storying tasks. Early users of Chronological Bible Teaching first shared teaching chronologically organized groups of biblical content lessons as *Phases*: Phase 1, Old Testament, Phase 2, the Gospels, Phase 3, Acts, etc. My Filipino storying mentor shared these as a mix of biblical content and as tasks: Evangelism, Review, Church Planting, Discipling, and End Times. Beyond the basic evangelism and church planting several additional tasks have been listed for the sake of planning and organizing the Bible teaching.

When the Bible Storying methodology, as used and taught today, was being developed I felt that *Track* was a more appropriate term to describe the groups of stories. So a track like the Evangelism Track consists of all the stories typically included in the teaching, along with any teaching/learning activities that are appropriate for the evangelism objective and for the significant worldview characteristics of listeners. Incidentally, we never refer to these "tracks" when teaching our listeners. The terminology is simply for our convenience in sharing the methodology and for our planning objectives and preparation of Bible stories and lessons.

Some new to Bible Storying have questioned why bother with tracks at all. Why not just tell the stories? This is fine and many do it intuitively with success. The concept of tracks serves the dual purpose of delimiting our focus in planning the stories and accompanying lessons, and in organizing or grouping the stories that serve to reach the objectives. The Evangelism Track usually deals with certain worldview issues that are not the same as those for planting a church or discipling new believers.

Later in telling the stories in the storying sessions we do not make reference to the tracks: "Now we are going to tell the Evangelism Track," or "now we are moving on to the Church Planting track." Instead, we just move to the next track of stories or continue with suitable bridging from the previous track of stories. Of course, if the story set is short or complete in one track then obviously this division is not needed for planning and preparation.

As a beginning Bible storyer you will be most concerned with the Evangelism Track. Later we will look at some other possibilities for using Bible stories which may better fit your personal or ministry needs.

First, a look at the five basic strategic tasks which I have referred to as *Tracks* or groups of Bible stories that serve an objective leading to Evangelism and Church Planting.

Evangelism Track—Generally beginning with Creation and covering key Old Testament stories expressing accountability to God, the broken relationship due to sin, God's judgment and punishment of sin, the promise of One to bless all peoples, a Substitute Sacrifice provided by God, God's Commandments to define sin, the need for an intercessor, stories of the persistence of sin, and finally the prophecies of the coming Promised Messiah. In addition there are commonly added stories that deal with various worldview issues that affect attitudes and receptivity of the other Bible stories.

The stories continue in the New Testament with the birth of Jesus in fulfillment of prophecy, stories that characterize Jesus as having authority to forgive sin, to heal, over nature, over evil spirits, and over death itself. Other stories deal with the arrest, trial, crucifixion, burial, resurrection, and finally the ascension. The actual stories used vary according to the preexisting knowledge of listeners, where they are spiritually and various issues related to their worldview and listeners' prevalent religion.

Review or Affirmation Track—This is a review of the key or central stories containing the truths leading to salvation. There are several reasons for reviewing these stories before moving on. First is the value of review with oral learners. They have heard the evangelism stories several times, perhaps over a long interval of time. In hearing the stories it was a progressive revelation for most as they did not know what was going to happen next or much later in the stories. Now, after they have heard all the evangelism stories from beginning to end, this is an opportunity to retell the key stories more quickly and use the teaching/learning time to connect and relate the beginning stories with the later stories as fulfillment.

For those who have made a decision to believe on Jesus as their Savior, the review of key stories is an affirmation they have made the right decision. The reason that only the key stories are told is because the worldview-related stories that were necessary to capture their attention, address spiritual errors, and provide affirmation through the bridging stories are generally less needed now. However, if a majority percentage of the listeners have not made a profession of their faith in Jesus, then it might be wise to retain some of the most significant worldview-related stories to continue challenging them.

Another very important reason for this Review Track is that it gives slow responders an extended second chance to profess their faith in Jesus. And for those who joined the listening group late the review of the key Old Testament stories gives them the needed background for their understanding of why God sent Jesus to suffer and die. Before proceeding with planting a church it is important to make every effort to bring all the listeners to faith in Jesus so that those who are merely interested will not be swept into the new church along with the believers. In communal societies it is difficult to exclude people from assemblies as this has great social significance and possible later consequences. The next Bible stories will be addressing believers and modeling for them what the believers did in the days following Jesus' return to heaven.

In actual field practice storyers have learned that often during this review track many of the listeners will in turn be sharing the stories with others. Some will begin their own storying sessions. This is well to encourage happening.

Church Planting Track—Beyond bringing oral learners to a salvation decision is the progression to gathering the new believers and providing a "church" model for them. A number of the Acts stories provide the needed model of the new church that formed among those who followed Jesus. There are a number of tasks embedded in these stories: worship, prayer, breaking of bread together, stewardship, leadership, ministering to those in the fellowship of believers, evangelizing those being drawn by the Holy Spirit, and sending out of missionaries. In addition there are several stories that clearly illustrate the baptism that followed believers' professions of faith in Jesus.

In addition to these Acts stories, it is helpful to include other stories that provide the background for the Lord's Supper, a review of the meal Jesus had with his disciples, what he taught them about the elements, and perhaps a look ahead at what Paul wrote to the Corinthian believers. Even a look back at the Hezekiah revival of the Passover conveys the preparation, the joy, and the worship of the observance.

Discipling or Characterization Track—In a sense these terms are arbitrary labels for our purposes in organizing and preparing stories and teaching/learning activities. I have used both track terms interchangeably. Both terms describe the function of this next set of narratives and lessons. The basic purposes are to: stabilize the new believers in their faith, to begin or continue the maturing of believers as they learn more about what is expected of them as followers of Jesus, and to help them have a helpful testimony for others among their people who are not yet believers. Characterization refers to learning to live a life that is pleasing to God and a strong testimony to their society of what it means to be a follower of Jesus. I used the reference in 1 Thessalonians 4:1.

End Times Track—Again, as in the other tracks, there are several reasons for the last group of stories needed to complete a basic study of the Bible. For those who are hearing the Bible orally and who cannot read it for themselves, these narratives provide closure to the Redemption Story. In fact, for some in the Islamic world these stories may be needed even in the Evangelism Track to deal with some of their beliefs regarding the End Times and ultimate salvation. The End Times narratives provide for the believer the coming victory and state of blessedness for them. For the unbelievers it is a final warning of the fate awaiting them. And for those who live in fear of the unseen malevolent spirit world there is the final punishment of the evil spirits and their leader. While much of the narrative comes from the Book of Revelation, there are other narratives from the Old Testament prophecies, the teachings of Jesus, and the Epistles that deal with the End Times.

So the people we teach never see this organizational structure. These divisions are for the purpose of the storyer's dividing up the tasks so that groups of Bible stories may be chosen to teach toward and focus on an objective. In my experience the two most often used tracks are the Evangelism Track and the Discipling Track. As the Bible storyer progresses, he/she follows a simple bridging or progression method from track-to-track without calling attention to the divisions. We are just continuing our study of the Bible.

By organizing the biblical teaching this way it is relatively easy to follow the timeline of the Bible and to accommodate the several tasks of introducing the Gospel, evangelizing, planting a church, and discipling new believers. There are some shorter strategies that incorporate all this into a single set of stories. This is fine. The larger strategy had its birth in working among those who live in communal settings where it is definitely an advantage to proceed at a pace which is comfortable for oral learners and to expose as many as possible to the same teaching to prevent persecution. It must also be comprehensive enough to reach a "tipping point" where the stories begin to make sense and displace their existing beliefs, to give as much of an Oral Bible as possible in the process, and not so lengthy as to cause major fading of the first stories before reaching the last stories.

Again, for many who are considering Bible Storying for the first time, there may be greatest interest in only the evangelism objective. This is fine. Among many of the rural pastors that I taught the stories, their first priority was to use the stories to disciple their people, many of whom knew little about Jesus, or even why he had to suffer and die. Still others reading this manual may have a ministry objective where Bible stories would be used during disaster response, relief ministries, development projects, or even personal counseling and comforting. Some even use selected story tracks for pre-evangelism or for probing for responsiveness. I have done this many times by proceeding through mainly the Evangelism Track stories, told continuously without pausing for reflection or discussion. This was done as a way to lay the whole story out before a people to see if there were interest in hearing again in greater detail and having opportunity to discuss the stories. This particular strategy is called Fast-Tracking the Story. More on these alternative strategies of use in a later chapter.

Fig. 2 Overview of the Church-Planting Phase and Tracks

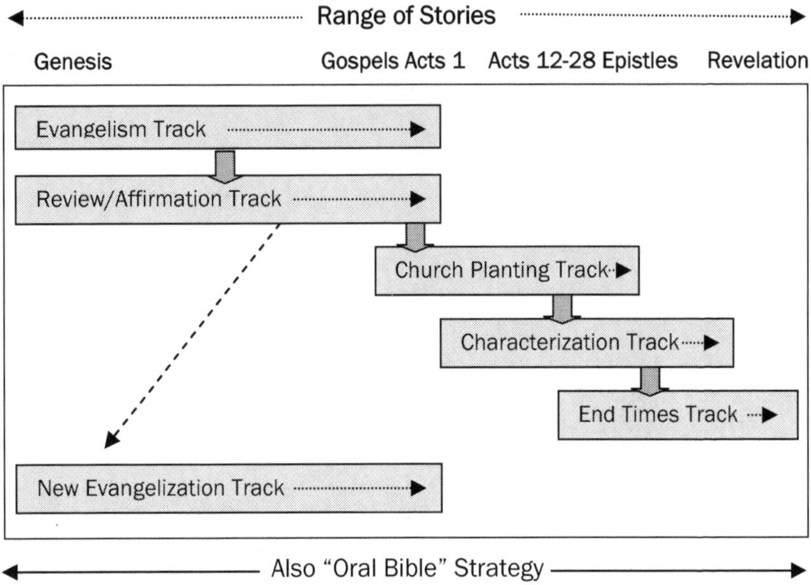

In ideal situations among receptive listeners some have simply merged the Evangelism and Church Planting into a continuous track and the followed with a Discipleship Track. Dividing the stories into tracks just makes it easier to select stories and focus on learning objectives in the discussion times.

Evangelism and Church Planting Phase—When developing Bible Storying as a methodology to suit Asian regional needs beyond the Philippines, the term *Phase* was chosen to describe the group of the various teaching tracks just described. The chart depicts the tracks, their range of stories, and their relationship to one another. This is not a hard and fast model to follow. It represents an ideal storying ministry that covers most needs. Each Bible storyer will in reality work out his/her own track strategy based on his/her ministry and people group needs.

Related to the Evangelism and Church-Planting Phase is the deliberate strategy to provide an Oral Bible for a people having no Bible in their spoken language or lacking the literacy to read and study the Bible. I'll discuss this more fully in a later chapter.

In the same way one may teach through the whole range of Bible stories or a limited group of stories arranged either chronologically or thematically for the purpose of further discipling and maturing believers, training new leaders and evangelists, preaching for oral learners, Sunday school lessons, ministry to believers and nonbelievers, and for training new Bible storyers. In Asia I had referred to these *beyond the Church-Planting Phase* as the *Church-Strengthening Phase* as all these possibilities for continued use of Bible stories contribute to a further strengthening of the new churches.

The basic idea is to continue with the stories to refresh them for oral learners, to add new stories that fill in the gaps or help to reinforce needed areas of faith and practice, and to train workers. Church-Strengthening tracks will also need to be sensitive to worldview issues that can affect understanding of the continued teaching, and putting it into practice. Let me remind that the terminology being used to present this methodology is for the sake of literate training and sharing among missionaries and other church workers. We don't use these terms with the people we are teaching.

As a beginning Bible storyer most will be more interested initially in the Evangelism Track stories (and possibly continuing through the Church-Planting Track stories), and in some shorter lists of evangelism stories suitable for use on short-term mission trips or in relief ministries. Do not be overly concerned about having to understand all the story track strategies. This larger framework is there as a strategy for those who need it. The basic Bible-Storying practice of telling selected stories for witness and ministry is pretty straightforward and easy to accomplish with the following thoughts about having a Bible truths list, knowing key worldview issues, and some basics of story crafting and presentation opportunities.

Fig. 3 Overview of Church Strengthening Phase and Tracks

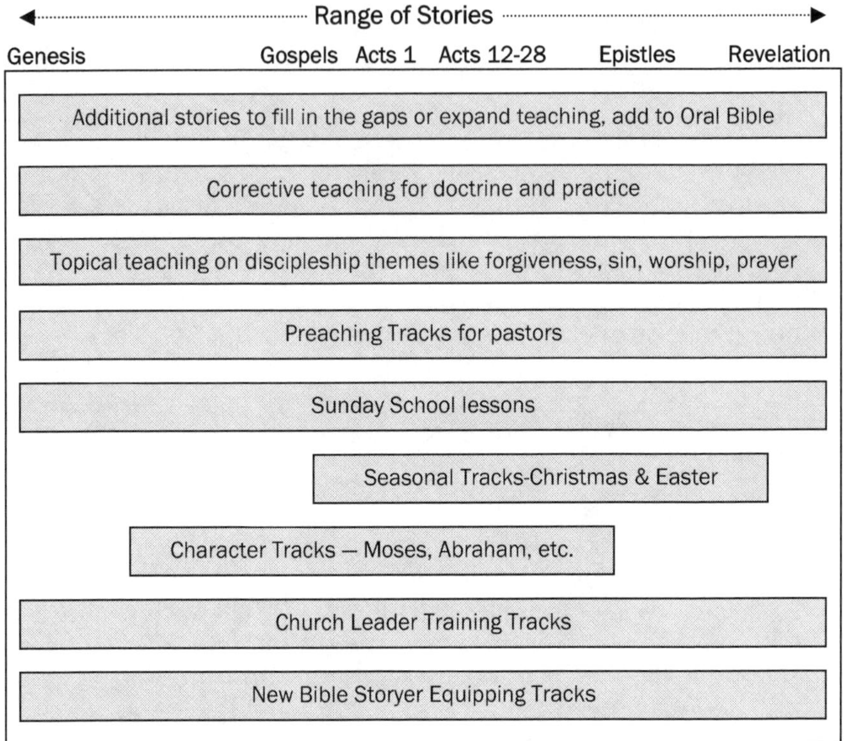

jot

The national co-workers that I taught and trained were most interested in being evangelists, discipling their people, and having a good supply of sermon components for their preaching. I felt it more important for them to know the Bible stories and to be familiar with teaching from them than to know many strategy possibilities which may have been difficult for them to duplicate or sustain over long time periods.

So I just taught the stories as groups of stories without ever going into any detail about the organization or structure I was using to plan and present the stories. Those I worked with learned the stories and just kept the same or similar organization as I had modeled for them. And some felt freedom to modify the story lists and even to re-arrange some of the stories to fit their own needs and applications among their people.

Chapter 5
Getting Started: Basic Bible Truths

Selecting the best Bible stories requires a basic outline that contains the truths needed to bring about the desired understanding and decisions. This selection is most important as Bible stories are not chosen at random, or simply from among those we like to tell (and remember), or even among the favorites of the listeners. The selection of stories stems from the spiritual truth the listeners need. Providing this list of the essential truths that the stories must teach is, therefore, a critical matter in the process of storying.

Early in the implementation of Bible Storying, teachers used a list of stories that had already been preselected by previous Bible storyers. Three Bible truth lists were in general use.

One approach listed *Six Characteristics of God* which served as a basic indication covering God's righteousness, his power, his knowledge, his grace, his hatred of sin and judgment of sin, and his promises. This list was popularized in the *God and Man* lesson model.[5]

Trevor McIlwain, from New Tribes Mission, shared a basic list that included the characteristics of God, man, Christ, and Satan. The model which provided a basic model for me came from another New Tribes missionary in a West African country.[6] Following is a suggested list of typical basic (sometimes called universal) Bible truths which can serve as a guide for choosing Evangelism Track stories.

Basic Bible Truths Leading to Salvation
(Evangelism Track)

1. God is one God, Sovereign, Creating, Present, and Acting in history.
2. God is all powerful, all knowing, the source of all grace, and provision for all a person's needs.
3. God communicates with people by His Word. He is faithful to his Word.
4. God loves all people and wants fellowship with them.

5. God is holy (separate from His creation), righteous in all He says and does, hating sin.
6. God's righteous nature demands that all sin be punished by death, which is eternal punishment (separation from God).
7. People are accountable to God for all they say and do, and are held accountable for obeying all God's commandments.
8. All people are sinners by inherited nature (birth) and by freewill choice, and are separated from God by their sin.
9. People can do nothing to save themselves from God's judgment and ultimate punishment for sin.
10. One can approach (have fellowship with) God only through the means God has provided through a perfect (sinless and acceptable) substitute sacrifice (Promised Anointed One who suffered and died in our place).
11. Jesus the Son of God (the Promised Anointed One come from God) is the only perfect sacrifice for sin.
12. Salvation for all people involves confessing that one is a sinner, turning from sin, seeking God's mercy in forgiveness of sin, and trusting through faith God's provision for salvation by believing on Jesus as the only Savior from eternal punishment for sin.

The Evangelism Track Bible Truths list is an important but not exhaustive grouping. Other suggested resource lists exist for Church Planting and Discipling. These lists are given in "Bible Storying Helps" in the back of this book. These lists are called resources because not all the truths listed may need emphasis in every situation. The storyer would certainly be free to develop his/her own list which he/she feels better states or covers what the listener group needs.

The longer lists of basic truths for the other tracks are shared as resources in an effort to be comprehensive but not exhaustive. A realistic working list would be much shorter and perhaps could combine several of the truths into one general statement as I have done in the preceding list for evangelism to keep it shorter and yet reasonably complete.

The need for emphasis of any one or all the basic truths is also related to significant spiritual worldview issues that are common for your listeners. For example in Christo-animistic societies where there is already some understanding about God and one's relation to Him, it is less necessary to deal with establishing the sovereignty of God and His relationship to mankind than with a typical Buddhist listener. So these basic truths in this list or in the list you compile will similarly reflect the realities of the spiritual worldview of your listeners: where they are in their spiritual journey and the truths they need to hear to come to an understanding regarding salvation.

Chapter 6
Getting Started: Core Bible Story List

Getting started is critical. One of the most commonly asked questions from those desiring to begin Bible Storying is: What are the basic stories I should tell? One of the major purposes of making a list of the Bible Truths the group needs is to have a criteria for selecting Bible stories. Once the storyer determines a list of basic Bible truths, it is fairly straightforward to select a list of Bible stories that teach or provide an opening for teaching those basic truths.

The concept of this list came about from observation during the pioneering days of Bible Storying development that certain key or core stories were used over and over again. These stories had originally been selected intuitively because they addressed the needed Bible truths. Later we will investigate the needed variations in this basic list of stories.

This basic evangelism story list could be used in most places with only minor variations. It is a list of stories I would feel comfortable in using as my basic list of stories if I were sent to a people that I knew little or nothing about their significant worldview issues. Note that the list is not exhaustive and it could be shortened even more as some of the basic truths are carried in more than one story.

The concept of a basic or core list of stories especially for evangelism was modeled in several earlier references. One such model came from Jacob Loewen's account among the *Chocos* of Panama. It listed twenty-six stories beginning with a story about the Origin of Satan and ended with the Ascension of Christ.[7]

A second model came from the Dell and Sue Schultze's *God and Man* lessons for the *Ilongots* of the Philippines. This model listed thirty-four stories that begins with God Revealed in Creation and ends with Jesus Christ the Promised Descendant is the True Lamb of God and High Priest.[8]

A third model was David Rodda's story list for Muslims of West Africa. He listed twenty-five tier 1 stories beginning with Where the Bible Came From and ending with Jesus Rose

Again, Appeared, and Ascended.[9] Rodda's list was unique in that he had four tiers beginning with "must-tell" stories and adding tiers of helpful or sometimes needed stories.

From my experience the following was the original list of core stories for evangelism:

Core Bible Stories for Evangelism

1. Creation of the world
2. Creation of man and woman
3. The first sin and judgment of Adam and Eve
4. Judgment of a sinful world in Noah's day
5. God's promise to Abraham of One to bless all peoples
6. God provides the substitute sacrifice for Isaac
7. The Passover—the blood and the Lamb
8. God gives His holy Law—the Ten Commandments
9. The Sacrifice System—shedding of sacrificial blood to cover sin
10. The Prophets' messages warning people to repent and the promise of a Redeemer who would suffer for man's sin
11. Birth of Jesus according to prophecy
12. Baptism and Temptation of Jesus—"Behold the Lamb of God," testimony of John and the Holy Spirit
13. Jesus and Nicodemus—"You must be born again"
14. Jesus has authority to forgive sin—Paralyzed Man and Four Friends
15. Jesus has authority over nature—Calming the Sea
16. Jesus has authority over demons—Gadarene Demoniac healed of evil spirits
17. Jesus is the resurrection—Jesus raised Lazarus to life
18. Abraham, Lazarus and the rich man—Man must believe the message of the Prophets in this life

19. The Last Supper—"This is my broken body and blood shed for you"
20. Jesus is betrayed, arrested, falsely accused, tried, and sentenced to death
21. The Crucifixion, decision for and against Jesus, "It is finished"
22. The Resurrection and appearance to disciples and followers
23. Jesus returns to the Father, the Ascension

--Following are optional stories for certain Asian spiritual worldviews--

24. Jesus the true High Priest (Hebrews 8-9), an advocate before the Father making intercession for believer's sins (Rom. 8:34; Heb. 7:25)
25. Return of Jesus to receive believers unto himself, to judge and punish unbelievers, Satan and the evil spirits, thus fulfilling all promises and prophecies.

This core list has several places where substitutions of similar stories are possible depending upon the listeners. A later expanded list added stories about the Bible and the Creation of the Spirit World which storyers discovered were needed among many animistic peoples, and additional stories which included testimonies of who Jesus is, especially for the Muslim world.

Another excellent evangelism story list is that provided by The Storying Scarf. This list of twenty-one stories can be accessed at www.StoryingScarf.com. This list, originally developed for use among Muslims of West Africa, also has been used among Spanish speakers of Central America. A similar but longer list of 42 stories comes from the Maasai people and is shared in the CESA Kanga Storying Cloth.[10]

One of the values of a core list of stories is that it provides a shortcut to beginning Bible Storying until the Storyer can develop a more relevant list. The storyer, however, should not limit himself/herself to only these example lists.

For a Church-Planting Track the core stories come primarily from Acts 1-12. Some additions, however, spring from later chapters and give examples of baptism. Still other examples come from the Epistles and give references to the observance of the Lord's Supper. For a suggested list of these stories see "Bible Storying Helps" (*see appendix*).

Defining a universal list of stories for discipleship and leader training is somewhat more difficult. LaNette Thompson has provided an excellent short list for discipling in her *What Jesus Wants His Disciples to Know and Do*.[11]

The Core Story List will later be modified or informed by key issues known about the intended audience's worldview which may point to preferred stories to tell or even those stories which might be skipped until later when there is more openness and understanding to accept them. The story list and its presentation as stories in Bible Storying sessions will be further influenced by other factors and strategies to be discussed in following chapters.

A very thorough and lengthy list of stories may not fit the time frame the storyer has with listeners. As that time frame is shortened the choice of stories becomes more critical. The ideal story list assumes that the time frame is not a limiting factor. When the list gets shorter it is usually best to increase the ratio of Gospel to OT stories.

In actual teaching it is not unusual to find that some stories did not work as well as anticipated to teach needed Bible Truths and other stories may be needed. Also it happens that some Bible Truths may already be understood by listeners so fewer related stories are needed. Still other truths may require additional stories to bolster the teaching. So the Core or Basic Bible Story List is only a beginning point that will be adjusted as needed, substituting, adding or dropping stories.

A continuing tension exists between those who favor a long and thorough teaching track with many stories and others who favor a shorter more generic teaching track that can be completed in less time and which may be more reproducible by non-literates. Longer gives more time for understanding and decision, shorter can be more expedient and urgent as well as memorable and reproducible.

Chapter 7

Getting Started: Considering Worldview

When the chronological teaching methodology was first shared with other missionaries, the fact that thought of worldview issues had gone into the story lessons prepared for use among Philippine listeners was evident. The original story models were, however, shared "as is" and attempts were made to use these models in other Asia countries where the local worldview was vastly different from that in the Philippines.

Early results were disappointing and generally failed to produce the desired interest or results among these new listener groups. When storyers attempted to discuss the stories after telling them, it was soon evident that many of the stories in the shared models failed to address critical spiritual issues. In addition, some of the stories in the way they were introduced, worded, and discussed were inflammatory among certain worldviews, particularly among Muslims. Additionally, evident gaps in the choice of stories caused critical issues to be ignored.

As an early storyer, I struggled to get a working hold on the significant worldview issues of those where I attempted to tell the Bible stories. Many issues were being discovered almost daily and some means was needed to make sense of their relevance and priority. About the time of this initial failure, two examples provided the needed concept. I was given a copy of a missionary meeting report from Japan which discussed the Japanese worldview as *bridges* and *barriers* to the Gospel.[12] In addition, New Tribes Mission shared a copy of the paper *The Ibaloi Barriers* which outlined in a simple format four major barriers to the gospel among the *Ibaloi* tribe of northern Luzon.[13] These sources suggested the needed direction and led to some basic methodology for organizing the needed information in a user-friendly format as bridges or barriers to the gospel.

The formal term commonly in use at that time was "Ethnographic Survey." Some of the ethnographic survey instruments led to a deluge of demographic information which did little to define Bible-story choices and spiritual issues needing attention. Over time an inventory of spiritual and related cultural worldview issue questions was devised and used along with a simple formula for exploring those issues which immediately related to the Bible-Storying process. In addition, an eclectic list of "Barriers to the Gospel" and "Bridges to the Gospel" was assembled from among many Asian worldviews and used as illustration in training conferences for missionaries. These lists can be reviewed in the "Bible Storying Helps" (*see appendix*).

A Simple Formula for Exploring Worldview Issues

The search for understanding of the Worldview issues is not complicated. In fact, the following guideline will give a simple formula for exploring understandings of a people's worldview.

1. *Explore the people's perceived needs.* Where do they see themselves as needy or lacking in their lives? This often points to openness for new information that will lead to changing their circumstances. Where there is perceived satisfaction there is greater resistance to change.

2. *Explore the changes occurring among a people*. What changes are occurring in their history, culture, beliefs, attitudes, fears, religion, safety, and political situation as it may relate to their national status? Among questions the storyer will approach should be:

    - *Changes in the past that could precipitate either openness to the Gospel or that further harden attitudes against the Gospel, the Bible, and Christianity. Also look for factors which may have led to a greater openness or expectation of future change as bridges.*

    - *Changes occurring at present which occupy listeners' attention and energy. These are generally topics of daily conversation and general interest in public, and over the local media.*

    - *Changes that are feared or impending that generate a climate of fear of outcome, upsetting of communal, social, or religious harmony are critical. In the same vein there are expectations resulting from dreams and other factors that provoke a desire to change, such as a desire for peace and harmony, education or literacy, safety, health, nutrition, and shelter.*

3. *Observe and note obvious Barriers* which are freely and openly voiced often by gatekeepers, religious, or political opinion leaders who seek to preserve their status and control. Some of these are traditional cultural and religious barriers that commonly exist while others may be more covert and embedded in their culture. Older people tend to be conservative, fearing change.

4. *Observe and note obvious Bridges* which are freely expressed most often by younger people, those dissatisfied with the status quo, or who have suffered a failure of their religion to fulfill their needs and so are open to change. One often finds among these groups persons ready to consider a new way and the new way can be the way of Christ.

Developing a Practical Working List of Worldview Issues

Several paths help in finding worldview information and putting the priority issues into a usable form. The lists of General Worldview Issues (Bridges and Barriers) in the Bible Storying Helps (*see appendix*) represent situations in many Asian cultures and were drawn from many Bible Storying situations and training sessions. In reality many more specific issues and shades of issues exist among a people. Be aware of this information and then process it into a usable form. Some typical ways to gather the needed information are:

1. *What is obvious and already known* (or suspected) among a people about their beliefs, religious rituals, and understanding of the relationship to the seen and unseen worlds? To whom or to what authority is mankind ultimately accountable? What is sin and what effect does it have on people? What are sin's consequences? How does one make it right after wronging another? Write down what is known and add to the list from continued observations.

2. *What has already been written* regarding the people

group? Are there some educational studies to reference? These often contain a wealth of information even when connected with secular studies—birth rituals, death rituals, agriculture, festivals, family structure, their religion rituals for worship, and means for seeking help from the deities. Some of my best initial information came from these kinds of sources. Check Internet sites (be sure to compare and weigh all sources as some sources are biased though may still contain useful information.)

3. *Plan to interview a wide variety of people from among the ethnic center*. These should include new believers (if there are any), unbelievers, men and women representing youth, married, and older adults. The older adults will be more conservative and knowledgeable of the customs and rituals of their people. Younger people will be more open and idealistic, curious, often desiring to experiment with change. Generally pastors and long-time believers are not as reliable a source for the needed information as their worldview may be more "Christian" than typical of the population as a whole. Don't overlook those who are hostile or gatekeepers who are opposed to Christianity or any change — hear their story, too.

4. *Have some informal discussion groups* in which the questions of life and spiritual issues are brought up. Talk about issues like power encounters, the source of blessing, how to restore broken relationships, and some general questions about life, death, and life beyond death. When someone wrongs you what is done: revenge, forgiveness, or restitution?

5. *Share and compare notes* with other Great Commission Christians working among the same people.

6. *Ask for some of the people's stories*. In this process, look for how they tell stories and how morals or other teachings may be embedded in their stories and passed along to the next generation. If there are collections of stories in books, read these as well.

7. *Compile the list*, collating issues which are related. One handy way to do this is to put the worldview findings on 3x5 cards and then sort them into categories. If a relational database computer program is available, use that.

8. *Prioritize the list* giving highest priority to those issues which obviously will affect openness and receptivity to Bible truth and ability to act on it.

This process should provide a list ranging from the most significant (as assumed at this time) to the least significant. The storyer can always update the list during or after telling the Bible stories, teaching the lessons, and getting feedback from listeners by their questions and from answers in the pre-story and post-story dialog sessions.

The worldview information will consist of a list of issues that may not at first sight appear to be related in any way at all. It is essential to look for general trends and characteristics and combine those issues that are similar or related through common roots. There will be issues that are beyond the purpose and scope to address. Simply be aware these exist but do not include them in the working list.

In a worldview study conducted among elderly Chinese widows in Singapore, a larger list of "One Hundred Objections to Christianity" emerged. The list was too large to use effectively. After lengthy study of the list, it was reduced to a list of ten basic worldview issues, all of which were barriers to Christianity, barriers to change, or which reflected a greater desire to be with one's ancestors wherever they are. Generally the issues which are priority issues are few in number. Others may be voiced but may be less significant and could be addressed, if not through the stories themselves, through the discussions about the stories, or perhaps later in discipling lessons or even some thematic storying tracks. What is important is to prioritize the list to the most significant issues that immediately affect the choice of Bible stories and the way the stories should be told to maintain a hearing.

There are three typical ways in which to confront worldview issues in the stories and lessons:

1. First is to directly *challenge* the issue head-on in an apologetic manner. Culturally this is not the best approach. The direct challenge method can work at times if the storyer has resources and a good relationship with his/her listeners. Most often, however, the method is difficult for a local storyer with limited Bible knowledge

and who does not organize his/her thoughts logically like a Westerner.

2. A second approach is to *by-pass* the issue until a later time when more stories have added to the weight of evidence that can challenge the issue. This often means some adjustment in vocabulary until the right time comes (ex: *descendants* of Abraham instead of *Israelites* used with Muslims—more on this in Crafting Bible Stories later).
3. The third approach is to *displace* the issues in error with a greater weight of truth. This may happen along the way without even bringing up the challenge to their beliefs as the weight of true stories mounts until a tipping point is reached. The storyer knows where the error lies and deliberately adds evidence against it. Change comes through the illuminating work of the Holy Spirit in listeners' hearts. Better stories will displace inferior ones if the better ones are more complete and relate better in logic understandable to the listeners. I have observed this happening when a listener began with: "If these stories are true then...." He had reached a tipping point.

In addressing worldview issues while moving through a chronology of stories, it is possible to stop and deal with a worldview issue topically if the question arises or if a teachable moment is sensed. Usually the best way to do this, while keeping to the chronology, is to reach back to earlier stories for truths and themes which address the issue in part or whole as a selective review, or add new stories previously skipped over by inserting them in the review. In selecting the list of stories it is possible to anticipate worldview challenges and add a series of stories which deal in greater depth with the issues in question. It is also possible to put off dealing with a worldview issue until more appropriate stories have been told in support of the change.

Worldviews are not static; they are constantly changing among many peoples due to increased access to foreign media programming, travel, educational influences, local failures of their religion, increased hardening and resistance to save their cultures, or to save their ethnicity or prevalent religion related to their nationality. In East Malaysia among the *Iban* people this happened when roads were cut through the jungle to their longhouses making access to the outside world easier. The old animistic rituals of the jungle began to give way to a more open and secular worldview brought in by those working on the outside and exposed to new experiences and value systems.

The worldview issue list can always be refined while teaching. Along the way it is not unusual to discover new and previously unknown issues that did not surface in initial investigation because the storyer is an outsider. But these new issues may slip out inadvertently as questions, comments, or other reactions in the course of discussing relevant stories. The really high priority worldview issues will manifest by the resistance, hostility, or general lack of understanding by the listeners.

A realistic working list finally should not contain more than 8-12 major issues (this is not a hard and fast rule). An inflated list of worldview issues will require a longer Bible-Storying track (three to five or more stories for major issues) to deal with them. So keep to the important issues. Look for any issues that can be put off and dealt with better in later discipling lessons rather than making them issues in evangelism. This is especially true among those where works-salvation concepts are strong.

At the beginning point mainly look for worldview issues that influence the receptivity to the Bible stories and teaching themes. Then while moving along in the Evangelism Track, be concerned with the listeners' comprehension of the major biblical truths regarding sin and God's promises about a Redeemer. If issues come up that stories haven't dealt with, put them off until getting to stories that address them. Don't jump ahead and attempt to deal with issues or answer questions listeners do not yet have a basis or preparation to understand.

Following is a list of worldview issues obtained for the *Grassroots People* of Hong Kong:

Obstacles (Barriers):

1. Sin—They see no relation between religion and morality.
2. Concept of God—The people have a concept of a Creator God but consider him aloof, unapproachable, and, importantly, uninfluenceable (this concept is the most usual view among traditional religionists).
3. Concept of death—The people believe that when an ancestor dies the person becomes a ghost that still has a relationship with the living. The deceased must be cared for and appeased to bring blessing to the family.
4. Group pressure—The people confront great pressure to conform to the norms of peers and the group: family, workmates, and their race.
5. Concept of themselves—Because of low income, education, and status the people see themselves as inferior with a natural fear and reluctance of meeting new situations.
6. Concept of coping—The people work hard to do the best they can so have little time for anything else. They are generally fatalistic in their basic outlook.
7. Concept of Heaven—They think the gods are in heaven. I want to be with my ancestors wherever they are, in hell, if there.

Gateways (Bridges):

1. Pay attention to power—The people give extreme honor to gods who fulfill their prayers. One has no relation with gods but only honors them.
2. Respect the older generation for their experience—The people are certain that this experience cannot be gained through schools or bought.
3. Place great emphasis upon immediate needs—The people have primary interest in the here and now. The distant past and unpredictable future have little importance.
4. Ritualistic People—The people live in a ritualistic society which provides a way to cope with life. Proper ritual holds a central and important place in their lives.

5. Insecure about the future—The people face sickness, accidents, loss of jobs, and other circumstances that lead to helplessness. They have no way to face the problems of life and death.
6. Need the warmth and care of a family life—Most of the people went to work at an early age or became caregivers so they lacked opportunity of a warm family life to nurture them.

The Bible storyer has the task of taking stories with a biblical worldview and presenting them to a people who may or may not have difficulty accepting the different worldview. The task is made even more difficult as the biblical worldview of the Bible is typically filtered through the storyer's Christian-Western worldview. Many unreached peoples live in cultures closer to an OT worldview which they may understand better than the storyer.

Next, what to do with this information once it has been gathered, collated, and short listed? The list of worldview issues will be compared with the list of basic truths to arrive at criteria for selecting Bible stories, influencing the crafting of the stories for telling, and the learning activities used to discover the truths to remember in the stories.

Remember that the worldview issues list will in one sense never be complete as new issues and facets are likely to be discovered. The priority and significance of worldview issues can shift as a better understanding is obtained through dialog, comments and observations. The worldview of the listeners will begin to change with the stories and other influences (like media and contact with those outside their culture) so it is not static.

Keep an updated list for sharing with the new personnel coming to work with you or for those to follow you. Some sets of model stories will have their worldview synopses or at least the most significant issues listed as a resource for the storyer.

Chapter 8
Choosing Bible Stories

Once the list of needed basic Bible truths is decided and a manageable synopsis of significant worldview issues are obtained, the criteria for selecting Bible stories is in hand. You will soon be aware that the number of stories is related to these criteria. If more truths and worldview issues are involved, the storyer will need to use more stories. However, many stories address more than one truth so there can be some compromise. Select stories where the needed truth is obvious and more likely to be picked up by the listeners.

The best procedure is to go through the Bible selecting the stories that address the basic truths to be taught. At this point it is helpful to be generous in choice of stories as the list can be pared down and refined later. The stories may either be selected chronologically or selected relationally at random and then put into a chronological order. Later, in looking at some other storying strategies, the possibility of organizing stories thematically or in some semi-chronological order will be addressed.

Then, with the short-listed and prioritized worldview issue list in hand, go back through the stories to see if additional stories will be needed for those difficult-to-accept truths, for major spiritual gaps that need to be filled, and for other stories needed to serve as bridges. Some of the more difficult-to-accept spiritual truths are those that challenge major beliefs of those in organized religions, those that may lead to persecution, or those that involve areas of animistic deep fear and superstition. Those challenges may require additional stories. Additional stories can serve to lead via some rational way into the major stories. These added stories can also serve as additional illustrations giving different perspectives, or give assurance that the outcome of any change will be beneficial. Let me illustrate:

Because of fear of disturbing the Spirit World and the powers behind it, a story addressing the Creation of the Spirit World can be helpful. There are options for this. In addition, multiple stories of Jesus' authority over the Spirit

World are usually helpful. Even the Job story can add weight to God's authority over Satan to limit his work.

Among Muslims the use of additional prophet stories can address the issue of sin—its persistence and consequences, as well as the fact that even prophets sinned.

In some Oriental worldviews there is a general belief that sin is a matter of killing and robbing. Some have suggested using more "small sin" stories so as to give a wider perspective regarding sin and its universality, and avoiding major stories that involve murder, at least early on in the story series.

In the "*E-etaow*!" video account of the *Mouk* people of Papua New Guinea, at one point in the teaching the people respond: "We are like that!"[14] The ideal is to have enough relevant Old Testament stories so that listeners can identify with the perilous condition of sinners. Then the following Gospel stories characterize Jesus as the Redeemer who has the compassion and authority to remedy the sinner's plight.

The Core Story list is helpful in getting started with its stories adjusted as needed according to the emphasis required. Substitutions can be made where several stories address the same or similar truths and issues. In developing story sets for Muslim women additional stories were added in which women were major characters like Rahab or Ruth, and where the choice of a story like the "Woman Who Anointed the Feet of Jesus" was the best example of Jesus forgiving a person's sin.

During the early years of Bible Storying a diagram served to depict the role of worldview issues and culture "informing and instructing" the choice of Bible stories, lessons, and teaching. This diagram served to contrast this preferred Bible Storying method to traditional evangelism presentations which were Bible-truth based but ignored cultural and worldview issues. The diagram was first shared in Lomé, Togo, so it has become popularly known as the Lomé "Y."

What is important to remember is that Bible story choices are deliberate and intentionally related to teaching objectives which facilitate the hearing and understanding by listeners. While this process may seem difficult to do at first, is becomes easier as the storyer works with a people group and develops an intuitive understanding of their spiritual openness and understanding.

Story choices are not set in concrete! It is not uncommon to make story changes in the course of teaching. It may be that certain stories land with difficulty on the ears of listeners, stirring their resistance and hostility. Other stories may provoke unintended responses by reinforcing unwanted behavior or raising questions that impede the teaching.

If the storyer observes these occurrences, story changes, either during the teaching track or certainly in the next teaching track, would be in order. Often the problem can be alleviated by changes in crafting the story or by adding additional stories that give a perspective to the offending story. We will discuss this idea more in "Story Crafting." After several times through a complete story set, the story list should stabilize and remain stable for future listener groups among the same people.

In addition to the question of what stories are needed, there is often the question of how many stories are needed? There is a general rule of thumb from practical experience. If a biblical truth challenges a particularly deeply entrenched worldview issue, as many as five to seven stories may be required.

For those truths that are in effect simply gaps in spiritual knowledge, or which address or challenge general issues, three or four stories may suffice. For those truths and issues which are more readily acceptable or less threatening to listeners, only one or two stories may do.

Do the math. If there are fifteen difficult truths to teach or issues to deal with, as many as sixty or more stories could be needed. If there is general agreement but simply lack of knowledge, as few as perhaps fifteen (or fewer) stories may do. Typically strategic evangelism story sets run from around twenty to forty stories with thirty-five being very common.

The Storyer will recognize that the process must be adjusted when working with people who are resistant to or hostile to Christianity, Christian groups or what is perceived as traditional Christian teaching. With persons who are resistant or historically hostile to Christian teaching it is better to err on the long side with a patient and carefully selected set of stories that carefully builds gradually gaining understanding and assent from the listeners. A series of related stories can often overcome hostility or resistance and open the way for acceptance. One of the great advantages of the Bible stories is their "coherence" and "continuity." Many of the organized religions have stories or reference to stories, some even similar in plot or theme to Bible stories. Many fragments of the Bible stories are, for instance, noted in the Quran. There are contradictions in story fragments as well. A carefully assembled set of Bible stories then deals carefully with bridging, joining and carrying over story threads that link the component stories to reduce the gaps or places where listeners can see a discontinuity.

Buddhism has its sacred scriptures as teachings in the Tripitaka and then various stories like the Jataka Tales of the Buddha. There is no sense of continuity.

Hinduism has more of a storyline in the Ramayana stories which detail the exploits of the characters but fail to have a coherent redemption theme for the listener. Other commonly used stories by Hindu storytellers are parabolic and teach various moral values.

Animists have their mythological stories which do not need to have any continuity. Each story is an isolated story often of a hero or to explain some occurrence and there can be discontinuity and contradiction from story to story.

These are just general comments to compare these other teachings and stories with the coherent nature of the Bible stories and overarching Redemption Story. It is a strength for the Bible storyer to utilize fully.

Following is an illustration of how the worldview and culture of listeners inform the choice of stories. These worldview and cultural elements also influence crafting stories, preparing accompanying learning/teaching activities, and presentation of the stories and learning/teaching activities.

Fig. 4 Lomé "Y" Worldview Helping Select Stories

Worldview Realities

- Perceived Needs that can open people to a relationship with God
- Their understanding of Accountability to God
- Worldview & Culture expressed as Spiritual Barriers and Bridges
- Their Language & Vocabulary

Lostness of People

Biblical Truths Leading to:

- Understanding accountability to God
- Understanding broken relationship due to sin
- Understanding helplessness to save themselves from God's wrath
- God's provision of a Substitute to suffer for sin
- Hearing Gospel as Good News of Forgiveness for Sin & Restored relationship with God through Jesus Christ

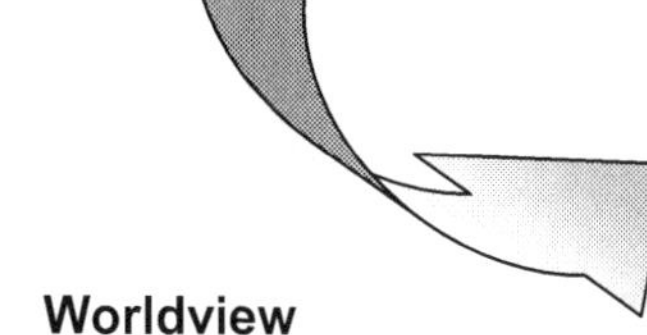

Understanding of their Culture & Worldview

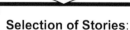

Consideration of their preference of Learning Mode—Oral Culture or Literate

Worldview

Informing Story Choice & Instructing Story Preparation and Teaching

Selection of Stories:

- *Driven* by Biblical Truth
- *Informed* by Their Worldview & Cultural Considerations
- Chronological or thematic arrangement to preserve historical & other biblical relationships

jot

Chapter 9

Crafting Bible Stories for Telling

The Bible is a wonderful book. It has been preserved and protected down through the centuries. It is good literature that reads well and for the most part tells well also. Why then should the stories be changed in any way for telling?

A number of reasons call for crafting or preparing the Bible stories for good comprehension when telling them to oral learners. These learners need to hear the stories so they can understand them and not be confused by details slipping by quickly in the narrative. They should not be left wondering about the details in the stories and their relevance or meaning.

Following are a number of observations from my experience in preparing and telling Bible stories. The list is not exhaustive but does reflect the major issues.

- Some of the stories are very long and may need to be compressed or shortened to a more compact length for telling. The Flood Story and the Ruth Story are examples.
- Some stories are very short and may need embedding in a larger story or have a framing story to set them up. The Two Hebrew Midwives Story in Exodus 1 is only two verses long and needs an introduction to bridge into it.
- Some stories contain significant amounts of numbers and geographical details which are important for a Bible student studying the story in great detail but which are confusing for oral learner listeners who do not have a frame of reference. Review the story of King Saul's sacrifice in 1 Samuel 13 and count the geographical names and numbers.
- In many stories there are different names used for God. The names of God may be less of a problem for Muslims but can be a problem for others like Hindus when just the name "the LORD" is used. Other names that are interchanged can be confusing as the Isra-

elites are also called Hebrews in the story above and beginning in Exodus.

- For the sake of not being redundant in stories many pronouns are used where we (literate believers) know who is speaking to whom. But for listeners, the character dialog may be unclear. This is very common in the four Gospels. It is easily remedied by replacing the pronouns with proper names even though this may sound clumsy and redundant to literates familiar with the stories.
- To make the character dialog more interesting reading, the words of the speaker are often interrupted by a reference of who is speaking. The Gadarene demoniac is quoted as saying: "My name is Legion," he replied, "for we are many." (Mk 5:9b). Generally it is helpful to precede dialog with the reference of speaker and the one being addressed, then follow with an uninterrupted dialog quotation.
- Some stories need a frame of reference that can be provided by a bridging story related to the main story and can be followed by follow-through stories that resolve the matter. These bridging and follow-through stories are usually needed to give the right perspective or to introduce relationships.

  The story of David and Bathsheba assumes a relationship between David, Uriah, and Bathsheba that is clarified in 2 Samuel 23 in an introductory story about David's bodyguards where both Uriah the Hittite and Eliam the son of Ahithophel are mentioned. Eliam is the father of Bathsheba and Ahithophel is her grandfather. (2 Sam. 11:3) Jesus' relationship with Mary and Martha (and Lazarus) is introduced in Lk. 10:38-42 before telling the story of the raising of Lazarus.
- Some stories work better in a cluster or told as one story with each component part bridged together. The parables were often told in clusters of three. A common thread or theme ran through the cluster — the rejoicing over finding the Lost Sheep, the Lost Coin, and the Lost Son.

- There are a few stories sometimes needed that are not found intact in one place in the Bible. All the story pieces are there but need to be gathered into a coherent narrative. A common one is a story about the prophets' words regarding the coming Messiah. A story related to the Creation of the Spirit World is another for animists.
- And for many, a story about the Bible, what it is, how it came to us, and what it has to say about itself as God's Word is a compiled story that may make use of both biblical references as well as nonbiblical history.
- In the course of telling many stories which teach the needed truths there are connecting, transition, or bridging stories needed to join one major story to another to bridge the time gap or to carry over a character or promise that continues. For evangelism, the Joseph story is often paraphrased into a condensed bridging story to get from the patriarch stories to the Exodus stories rather than to take the time to cover all the events in the life of Joseph.
- Some stories may carry details that are inflammatory or not socially acceptable to those who do not understand the overall Bible message. The Samaritan Woman at the Well story has posed problems for some when it is mentioned that the disciples left Jesus alone at the well while they went to find food. Could the disciples' departure be omitted in telling the story in order to keep the listeners' attention focused on the words of Jesus and the woman's response rather than a supposed social impropriety of the woman alone in a remote place with someone not her husband or family?
- Vocabulary can pose a problem as use of the term "Israelite" with some Muslim listeners. A suitable alternative is usually "descendants of Abraham." The term "Son of God" is also a problem and must be used with care though it seems to be possible when story characters are the ones who say it in their dialog.
- Some stories may need slight rearranging for greater

clarity and to make important comparisons. One example is that of the intertwined stories of the births of Ishmael and Isaac. In some cases it has proven wise to tell a composite story of the birth of Ishmael and his being sent away before returning to the story of Isaac. The Muslim listeners would expect the Ishmael story and need to hear it and then to hear the Isaac story in its entirety in contrast. Oral learners can have difficulty with parallel story tracks that intertwine rather than completing either one before beginning the other.

- There are many places where a story is implied but not explicit though there is sufficient descriptive detail and teaching to narrate it as a story. The Sermon on the Mount is an example.
- Be aware of how some stories end or where they end. At the end of the story of Deborah and Barak the enemy Sisera flees to the tent of Jael, the wife of Heber, because there is a friendly relationship between Heber's people and Sisera's king. Jael first offers hospitality and then kills Sisera as he sleeps. In the Middle Eastern cultures anyone who is under your roof is under your protection. But a man does not enter the quarters of a woman not his wife. Many listeners will forget the rest of the story and dwell on the ending that breaks cultural mores.
- And finally where multiple accounts of the same story with perhaps differing details exist like the Gospels, a harmonized story is possible that is more coherent and descriptive. In other places parts of a story may be explicit but are scattered over several books of the Bible like the Hezekiah Revival story ending with the threat against Jerusalem. These can be combined into one continuous narrative with several connected events.

Having said all of the above that actually comes from my own storying experiences, I must add that we are to treat the Bible stories with great care and respect. We realize that all translations are to some extent an accommodation to the literary norms of educated readers and that some of the cultural nuances are often lost in the translations from one language to another. For example are the many plays on words in the Hebrew language. Various grammatical devices and variety are used in English to make reading the Bible more interesting. Some of the items mentioned in the previous listing may in fact be taken care of in the local language translations. Learn to read the Bible with the ear of an oral learner.

Note also that the Bible writers were very sparse in their use of descriptives. There is some occasional stereotyping of characters like Ehud and Eglon in the Book of Judges, or in the use of terse comments regarding why things happened, or in summary regarding a person's character. Note the comments made regarding the evil done by many of the kings of Israel who were said to be "more evil than any before them," or that they "failed to walk in the ways of David." Differentiating between Elijah and Elisha requires care as does how to make the transition from Abram to Abraham. I have often found it easier to use only the name Abraham and to refer to his earlier name, that God changed it, and the difference in meaning with his new name.

In general, descriptives slow a story down and verbs speed a story up and give it energy. Character dialog is extremely important to oral learners. I learned the hard way that by removing most of the dialog from women's stories to make the stories simpler to tell and easier to remember I drained the life blood out of the stories. Women listeners enjoyed hearing the story characters speaking. Also I learned, that regarding some sensitive issues, the story characters could say things that I couldn't say directly in the way of comment or teaching. Testimonies about Jesus being the Son of God is one example.

The typical Bible story has a component of narration that introduces the story, its characters, and provides needed scene changes and transitions. There is the character dialog that usually carries the plot. Finally there is often a closing comment made by the narrator.

For illustration consider the story of Esau and Jacob in Genesis 25. The narrator describes the births of the twins and then compares them by stereotyping them as a father's boy and a mother's boy. The dialog begins when Esau returns famished from his hunting and demands some of Jacob's stew. But Jacob begins to bargain for Esau's birthright. Esau gives in to his physical desires and yields the birthright. Having told this, the story quickly moves to conclusion in a series of four verbs that succinctly describe the closing action. Esau "...*ate* and *drank* and then *got up* and *left*." (*Italics added*.) The narrator then steps back in with a closing comment: "So Esau despised his birthright."[15]

Character dialog would not be possible without the component characters. Generally there are three types of characters in Bible stories. These have been described as "round," "flat," and "stock" characters. Round characters are those undergoing change, growth or who are unpredictable. One might consider Simon Peter a round character as he changed in the course of the Gospel narratives. A flat character is one who is predictable or even stereotyped. Judas Iscariot is an example as are the Scribes and Pharisees who opposed Jesus. Stock characters are the onlookers, those in the stories like the multitude that Jesus fed who are not really characterized but play a role in the story. If you want to read more on this refer to the chapter on *Characters in Old Testament Stories* by Richard L. Pratt.[16]

Stories also make use of scenes or locations where the story takes place. Succeeding parts of the story may move from scene to scene. The Raising of Lazarus begins across the Jordan where John used to baptize, then shifts to just outside the village of Bethany where Jesus meets Martha, and finally to the tomb where Jesus raised Lazarus. Part of the dialog occurs in the transition from outside Bethany enroute to the tomb. The Gethsemane story takes place in the Garden but shifts back and forth from where the disciples are told to watch and wait, and where Jesus goes farther to pray alone.

Plot is the action line of the typical story. Description of the actions of the characters and their dialog carries the plot. Some narrated Bible accounts do not have a typical or well defined storyline but is basically static in that dialog or discourse occurs without the typical action plot. For oral learners even these non-typical stories may be narrated in story style. Think how you would tell what was said if you were there listening and watching it happen.

At this point you may be thinking these are too many things to consider. Don't give up. There are two simple basics. Ask yourself: Does the story tell well (smoothly)? And is the story understandable to the listeners? If not, then prepare to craft the story.

I had begun using the term "editing Bible stories" but this sounded too much like I was dissatisfied with the Bible and so changing it to say what I wanted it to say. One bottom line rule in story crafting is always to stay as close to the original wording as a good oral narrative will allow. A good text on preparing and telling near verbatim Bible stories is Tom Boomershine's *Story Journey: an Invitation to the Gospel as Storytelling*.[17]

For the listeners, understanding the story accurately is the key. The strategy is for Bible stories to be repeated by listeners so the stories may spread freely among the people group. To facilitate this, get the story as close as possible to the form that it will likely travel in to minimize listeners' editing the story by keeping the parts they are in agreement with or dropping the parts they don't understand. In the later chapter on "Problems, Questions & Answers" I will again mention negative restructuring of stories and story fading with the need for corrective refreshing.

Later in dealing with the actual telling of Bible stories it will be mentioned that a well-told story is dynamically recreated in the telling rather than regurgitated verbatim from memory. But this does not imply freedom to make drastic changes in the stories. Because these stories are structured for objective teaching and retention, there is not the freedom to dress up the story in an entertaining manner as might be done for literates already familiar with the stories and can read the actual verbatim story in their Bible.

If consideration of any of these matters is a problem, make it a matter of prayer to work out the stories so that you are comfortable with how to tell them. Reading from various versions like the Amplified Bible or the Living Bible or other conversational versions can be helpful in seeing how to express the story as a told story. I tell people to read the stories aloud ten or more times, close their Bible and then tell the story as you recall it. Record the story if you wish and listen as an oral learner who does not know the story. Is it coherent, does it flow smoothly, are there any difficult words or terms used that interrupt the storyline? When you fix these things, you have "crafted" the story.

Still, I will not be surprised when people ask: "How do you tell this story?" Next are some possible formats and illustrations of crafted Bible stories.

Chapter 10
Illustrations of Story Formats

There are many options for crafting or formatting Bible stories for telling. These depend upon the use of the story and upon the preference of the listeners. Generally a Bible story is crafted to make it easier to tell, easier to understand by the listener, easier to remember, and hopefully less likely to be restructured by listeners when they retell it. Each option has advantages and disadvantages that I will discuss briefly and provide illustrations of several for your comparison. Which one is best to use? That is your decision after considering the options.

Here is a listing of the many options a Bible story may be presented in:

- Verbatim (word for word) retelling from the local text. This method may be the best for use with conservative Muslims because no changes are made in telling to the story. It is the most accurate from a literate sense though it can be confusing and filled with difficult-to-understand items.
- Limited or Edited Verbatim in which original wording is retained as much as possible but with the option to leave out items to simplify or shorten the story to make it more manageable for listeners. This is still accurate but not as loaded with difficult-to-understand details.
- Crafted Bible Stories in which effort is made to preserve original or near original wording as much as possible but with intentional changes made to simplify the stories to better meet the criteria listed above. There are several forms of crafted stories including the basic story that is just simplified by making certain helpful changes to "oralize" a written story.
- Extended Stories are those crafted in which two or more stories are joined into a longer narrative to provide an entry story, the main story and one or more follow-through stories to bring closure. Very short

stories like that of the Two Hebrew Midwives in Exodus 1 benefit from being attached to or embedded in a larger narrative which provides a framing for their story. The David and Bathsheba story needs an introduction to establish relationships in the story and benefits from follow-through stories to illustrate consequences.

- Enriched or Composite Stories are those crafted stories in which two or more parallel accounts are merged into a fuller single narrative. This is a harmonizing of related stories in the Gospels like Feeding the Multitude and some of the parables. This is also possible with parallel accounts in the books of Kings, Chronicles, and Major Prophets. The Hezekiah Revival story benefits from this.
- Story Clusters are different from extended crafted stories in that there are several stories which are independent stories but share a common theme or thread like forgiving sin stories, healing stories, authority over evil spirit stories, etc. Other cluster examples are like the parables of The Lost Sheep, The Lost Coin, and The Lost Son, the Prayer parables, or even worship stories from the Old Testament. Other story clusters can compare characters and their traits. These classifications are not meant to be exclusive but simply help in defining some options for selecting and connecting stories for telling.
- Compiled or Synthesized Stories are those built into a narrative from components found in the Bible but not organized into an explicit narrative in one scripture passage. Three of the most commonly used compiled narratives are The Creation of the Spirit World, What is the Bible? and the Coming Messiah Prophecies. Some storyers are not comfortable in doing this with the Spirit World Story using the Isaiah 14 and Ezekiel 28 passages though it is widely used among animistic peoples to put to rest who is in charge of the unseen spirit world. If so, devise your own version.
- Paraphrased Stories are stories reworded by the storyteller into his/her own words. The stories may or

may not closely parallel the source Bible story. Many children's Bible stories are examples of paraphrased stories where difficult words are changed, some story reorganization may take place to simplify the plot, and in some cases the harshness of the source story may be softened or slightly refocused for the worldview of young listeners. There are two typical forms of paraphrased stories. These are my terms for the sake of differentiating them. First is the Lightly Paraphrased story. Second is the Deeply Paraphrased story.

- Lightly Paraphrased Bible stories are those retold more or less in simpler words, compressed into a summarized story, or possibly simplified in its organization without exaggerating any portion. It has no comment or teaching added into the story to expand or restructure it. This is common for stories used to bridge between major stories. And this is often the format used with stories for children.
- Deeply Paraphrased Bible stories are those stories in which extensive story restructuring is done to enhance teaching. It is always good to remember that anything added to a told story for oral learners then becomes "scripture" for them. Examples of restructuring include:
  - — the addition of copious descriptives,
  - — the mention of references to earlier or later stories as they relate to present events,
  - — adding teaching comments,
  - — the inclusion of explanation or application beyond that of a simple inserted explanation to clarify unusual items.
- Recast Stories take the paraphrasing a step further in that the story is relocated in time usually to the present or near present, the characters are changed to represent those like the listeners, and certain other changes may be done to "modernize" the story, or to change certain aspects of the story that may hinder listeners' accepting it for teaching purposes. The main

reason for recasting a story is to emphasize its relevance to the listeners by helping them to identify with it. These usually work best when coupled with the original Bible story told later.

- Chanted Stories are a form unique to many indigenous cultures where the stories are told in a poetic cadence. This is difficult for non-indigenous literates to do successfully. Non-literates' ability to learn the stories and chant them can grow out of repeated listening to verbatim recorded or read stories. Once when in the Chachuengsao area of Thailand, missionary Bob Stewart had one of his rural pastors to demonstrate a chanting of the Book of Genesis. After about fifteen minutes listening I agreed that he could do the whole book. It was a rhythmic presentation, all from memory.

- Sung Stories are very important to many indigenous cultures who like to sing them communally or while working in their fields. Sung stories usually are in one of two formats. One is a ballad format in which the storyline is sung ballad-style telling the storyline in song. Some songs can be quite long and may be performed by professional storyteller/singers among a people. An old Punjabi man at a storying training conference in Pakistan sang the story of Jonah in about fifteen minutes. On a night over in India two men told and sang that same story in around three hours.

  A woman visiting a missionary friend in a southeastern African country heard some women singing a very beautiful song in their language while working in the fields. After listening for awhile the visitor asked her missionary friend to come and listen and tell her about the song. After listening for a few minutes the missionary replied: "The song goes like this: If you boil the water, the children will not get diarrhea!" Health agencies often use songs to help oral communicators to remember important health practices.

- The other song format is that of verses with refrains which divide the story into segments, episodes, or may sing about the characters and their characteristics. In many countries the listeners join in the refrains. One of the missionaries in Togo shared an anecdote in which she criticized her pastor for writing while she was telling the Bible stories. He explained that his people remember important things in story form, so he was putting her told stories into song for his people. Then the pastor added with a wink: "Keep telling the stories because you don't sing very well!"

- Dramatized Stories are those told in any of several dramatic forms. One of the major advantages is the visualization of the story for the viewers. In many cases dialog must be added or expanded and a narrator may be needed to explain certain things which cannot be easily visualized. Dramatized stories work best when they follow a well-told story which closely follows the biblical account. The New Tribes missionaries telling the stories to Bisorio peoples in Papua New Guinea used such stories with great effect.[18] Other examples are like the Thai ligay that has been popular for use by Christian groups in Thailand.
- Puppet Presentation is a special form of dramatized stories in which the story is visualized by the puppets that may be speaking dialog that would be offensive or incite hostility if "spoken by the missionary" but since the words are coming from a puppet they are accepted. In many indigenous cultures puppets are not considered "just for children." Puppet presentations preserve cultural heritage, especially in Indonesia with the wayang kulit shadow puppets.
- Danced Stories are very important in a number of cultures as a part of their folk culture in which their heritage or religious stories are danced. The stories are generally well known by the listeners and the dancing provides a visual interpretation of the stories. A missionary couple in Bali was learning the basics of Balinese dance so they could dance the stories in a form that is greatly enjoyed and appreciated by the Balinese. In Madras, India, a dance company has specialized in dancing the Gospel stories. Obviously

this requires those who are part of the local culture to perform.

- Mixed Folk Media combinations of the above formats are found among many indigenous peoples. In the Philippines the zarzuela is a song and narration enactment. Among the Kui of the Khond Hills of India there is a das katha song and dance recounting of stories by two men to the accompaniment of rhythmically clicking two sticks together. One group in Bangladesh has used what might be called a Bengali cantata to present an all night story of Jesus in narrative, drama, song, and dance to Muslims. When Bible stories are introduced into these media the stories become very attractive to listeners and may travel far and wide as a folk media presentation.

Obviously some of these formats are nearly impossible for an outsider to perform without intensive cultural study and ability. But if the Bible stories can be told so that the stories can enter the cultural forms, then the stories will be attractive and largely memorable to listeners. The major drawbacks are exaggeration of stories in the telling or performance, or influence and contamination from other historical and mythical stories present in a culture.

Highly important for the beginning Bible storyer are:

- *the Bible stories likely to be told by the storyer for evangelism or discipling*
- *and how to format them for best understanding. Now for some illustrations.*

Verbatim Bible Story

Go to 1 Samuel 13 and read the story of King Saul's disobedient offering of the sacrifice. Only a priest was authorized to offer or officiate a public sacrifice. Read the story aloud and mentally think about all that is in it. You will be reading many numbers, including some large ones. The characters are King Saul, his son Jonathan, the Prophet Samuel, the unnamed soldiers, and the Philistines. Do you think that hearing the two different words for the Israelites might be confusing to a listener—"Hebrews" in vs. 3 and "Israel" in vs. 4? How many different geographic locations are mentioned? Is it helpful for you to know these while telling the story? Do you think it would be helpful for your listeners who have no knowledge of Palestine to be left to figure out where all these places are? Though the biblical division ends at 15, the actual story ends at 14 where it ends on an important word regarding future events.

In practice I have found stories like this can easily be edited by dropping out the items that factually load the story but contribute little to the movement of the plot. But if I were with Muslims I would be very careful with stories about Abraham and especially those where Ishmael is involved to minimize the accusation that Christians alter God's Word. In some places Muslim listeners may actually listen better if the verbatim story is read as they are accustomed to their teachers reciting out of the *Quran*.

The Flood Story covers four chapters plus a few verses in Genesis 5 where Noah's father and siblings are mentioned. There are again details which might be left out like the many numbers, some of which could be put into more visual wording listeners would grasp more easily—"after a long time had passed": instead of the recounting of 7 days, 40 days, 150 days, and another 40 days and 7 more days plus the references to the days and months. The actual ark dimensions are likely not helpful in telling the story—"God told Noah how large to build the ark." The three times that it is mentioned that Noah did everything the Lord commanded him is important as a thread or theme that carries through the story.

Once when telling this story to some *Marwari* tribal people in Pakistan I deliberately left out the part about sending out the birds at the end in order to streamline the story a bit. Later I was severely chastised by an elder who pointed out to me that birds were very important in his culture and were omens of good and evil. He said that when the white "pigeon" returned with a leaf, Noah knew that God's anger had passed, and now it would be peaceful, and Noah could come out of the ark. In his culture a string of leaves over their home doorways is a sign of peace for all who enter. I am careful about telling that story now!

The Joseph, Ruth, and Esther stories are too long in

general to be used verbatim. Jonah is borderline at four brief chapters. So this is a general disadvantage of some verbatim stories. By dropping out portions and perhaps connecting the main parts, a compact narrative will result where the story line is not lost in the wealth of details while the listeners are struggling to understand their relevance.

Crafted Stories

There is not a hard dividing line between where a limited verbatim story with light editing ends and a basic crafted story begins. The main criteria for considering crafting Bible stories is to make the stories into better oral narratives. Bible translators work toward accurate but literate wording which may or may not make good oral narratives. Paraphrased versions are by nature more oral in characteristics. This trend may be changing at least for initial translations.

Some of the common things altered in a basic crafted story are long discourses that may be edited down or summarized. Proper names instead of pronouns are used in the quotations when characters speak. Quotations should not be interrupted by speaker references. It is advisable to include the proper name of who is speaking to whom, even if it seems redundant to the storyer. Some occasional aside explanations might be used like John did in the Wedding at Cana story regarding the water pots. If more explanation is needed it should be made before telling the story. If expressions like "Israelite" are a problem for some listeners, instead use "descendants of Abraham." Be consistent in the names used for God. There are stories where "the LORD" is used with other names. To Hindu listeners, do these refer to other gods? Usually with Muslims this is less of a problem with Allah and appended characteristics, i.e., Allah the Merciful, etc. Items like the social situation where Jesus is alone with the Samaritan woman may indicate leaving out the departure of the disciples to buy food, their return, and Jesus' brief discourse on the harvest in order to move the story quickly from the woman's leaving Jesus to report to the town people, their response, and the powerful confession they make regarding who Jesus is.

Lightly Paraphrased Stories

These are most often used as introductory or bridging stories to get into main stories where you don't want to get into a lot of distracting detail before the main story. Paraphrased stories are used as transition stories where longer stories like the Joseph Story are telescoped into a summary that briefly touches only the high spots leading to Jacob's family moving to Egypt. This story connects the Patriarch stories to the Exodus stories.

There are other times when witnessing and a story is needed for illustration and there is not time for the full story. Then summarizing the story may give just the detail and emphasis needed. Paraphrased stories are used with children in order to simplify the story a bit, to slightly refocus some stories like the Flood Story from the harsh details of the flood judgment to focus more on God's goodness and provision in helping Noah to save his family and the animals. We don't remove the judgment theme, just subdue it a bit to focus on God's help and Noah's obedience for children's worldview.

Deeply Paraphrased Bible Story

Following is a story which illustrates some of the issues of this format. Early successful storyers used this format and it worked for them though it is presently discouraged in practice. Oral learners, who do not have access to Bibles nor literacy to read them, do not know what is "Bible" and what is "not Bible" in deeply paraphrased stories.

Cain and Abel: The Sons of Adam and Eve

Adam and Eve were commanded by God to multiply in order to fill the world with people. God is the one who gives us children, and He gave Adam and Eve their first child. The child was a boy and they named him Cain. While Eve was suffering from giving birth, she remembered the sin that separated them from God. When the baby boy was born, she remembered the promise of God— the promised Savior. Years passed and Eve again gave birth to another child. Again, it was a baby boy and they named him Abel. While Cain and Abel were growing up, Eve gave birth to several other children.

When Cain and Abel were already grown, they were taught by Adam and Eve that those who believed in the promised Savior would show this by the sacrificing of animal offerings. There should be blood shed and the death of an animal in exchange for the one giving the offering.

After they grew into adults, Cain became a farmer and Abel a shepherd. One day, they each gave an offering to God. Abel offered a sheep that he raised but Cain gave offerings from his farm. In your own thinking, did God receive their offerings? God only accepted the offering of Abel. Because of his faith, Abel offered an innocent sheep. There was blood in his offering. But God did not receive Cain's offering. Although there were two of them who offered sacrifices, God received only the offering of Abel. Why? The reason was because the offering of Cain was fruit of his own labor. God will never accept offerings made by man.

Do you still remember how God did not accept the clothes of leaves made by Adam and Eve? God did not receive the offering of Cain because there was no blood involved in it.

Cain got angry. God received the offering of his brother but his offering was rejected. God did not want to punish Cain along with Satan, so He admonished Cain. But Cain turned down the advice of God just like he turned down the teachings of his parents.

Cain was jealous of Abel; so one day he killed Abel. This was the first murder. Who do you think taught Cain to kill? God or Satan? Satan, of course, because God will not teach us to do what is evil or wrong.

This also teaches us that the sin of Adam was carried over to his children. Because of Adam's sin, sin will be the nature of everyone born. Consequently, all humans are sinners. All people are born sinners.

In your own understanding, did God see what Cain had done to Abel? Yes, because God can see everything that we do. Do you remember the question of God to Adam after he committed a sin, "Adam, where are you?" After Cain murdered Abel, God asked, "Cain, where is your brother?" Cain answered, "I do not know. Am I my brother's keeper?" God knew that Cain killed his brother because He knows everything. Nothing can be hidden from God.

God punished Cain for his sin. God told Cain that the land he was tilling would no longer be productive. The land that he was depending on would be cursed. Every time that Cain thought about farming, he would remember that his offering did not please God. Cain spurned the way of God and chose the way of Satan, and he did not change his thinking about sin.

Cain left his place and married one of his sisters. His family did not obey the way of God.

If we commit a sin, our sin is against God. For example, if a person tells a lie to his fellow man, his sin is not only against his fellow man but against God as well. Cain built the first city. Cain did not want the help of God in building the first city. He just trusted in his intellect, capabilities, and strength in leading the city. The children of Cain were also sinners like him. There was a man named Lamech who was a descendant of Cain. He married two women but God's plan is to have only one wife. Then one day there was a person who hit Lamech, and he killed the person. He boasted of the event to his wives.

All the descendants of Adam and Eve were sinners. Adam and Eve had several children. One of them was named Seth. Seth and his children followed the way of God. They called themselves the people of God.[19]

Following is a compiled story of the Creation of the Spirit World from Kristen Hoatson in Africa that was shared with me. It is very similar to many versions of this story in wide use.

God Creates the Spirit World

"In the beginning, when God created the universe, the earth was a desolate place. It was a dark, wild ocean of water. But in heaven, God created multitudes of spirits to worship Him and serve Him. He created all of them good.

God created one spirit to be especially wise, powerful, and beautiful. God gave this spirit the special job of guarding

His holy throne in heaven. But soon this spirit became filled with pride. He decided that instead of serving God, he wanted to take God's place in heaven and rule over all the other spirits God had created. He said in his heart, 'I will *ascend to heaven....* I will sit enthroned**....** I will make myself like the Most High.*'* He rebelled against God and many spirits joined him.

Because of God's great holiness, God could not allow that kind of rebellion in heaven. So He punished this spirit and all the spirits who followed him. God cast them out of heaven and put them on earth. And one day, God will send Satan and all the other disobedient spirits to hell, a place of eternal punishment which He created for them.

We know this spirit as Satan. The name Satan means 'adversary' and to this day Satan, and the evil spirits who followed him, try to destroy the good that God does and tempt people to sin against God. God's Word tells us that Satan is a deceiver, a liar, and a murderer. But God is more powerful than Satan. Satan can only do what God permits him to do.

Not all the created spirits went bad. Most of the spirits in heaven remained loyal and obedient to the God who created them. We know these spirits as angels. God used angels to speak his words of good news to people, to help people, and to warn about sin and punish people when they sin.

Although angels are very powerful, people are not to worship them. Like people, they are still created beings. They serve and worship God, who created all spirits and is the one and only ruler of the spirit world."[20]

In the accompanying lesson Kristen lists all the source scriptures used in compiling her story. There are other options for a Spirit-World story which do not make use of the Ezekiel 28 and Isaiah 14 passages. Some use the Job Story instead or a reference to the Witch of Endor story with Saul.

An example of a recast story is one recounted by Bill Musk.[21]

Two Men Who Went To Pray

"There were once two Muslim men who went to the mosque to pray. The first man was a devout Muslim who had been to Mecca on pilgrimage, prayed regularly five times a day, and was known in the community for his piety. He went to the mosque that day with total confidence, for he knew all the prescribed rituals of how to wash himself before entering the mosque, as well as the set movements and words of the prayers. He entered the mosque, went straight to a prominent place in the center towards the front, and performed his prayers with absolute perfection. But while praying, his thoughts wandered to the pretty girl who lived next door and he pictured to himself her shapely figure.

The second man to come to the mosque had lived a thoroughly rotten life of moral degradation. Having not prayed for many years, he had forgotten the details of the outward ritual of washings, prayer movements, and even the words one recited in prayer. But he was deeply aware of the evil of his behavior and longed to get right with God again, start a new life, and make amends for all he had done until then. Shyly he approached the mosque, dipped his hands in the pool of water to wash his hands and face, left his sandals outside the mosque, and slipped quietly in. Feeling a bit of out of place, he went behind a pillar in the hope that no one would see him. Deeply moved with a spirit of repentance, he abandoned any attempt to remember the set words and movements of prayers; so he turned to God with simple words of his own.

With which man's prayers was God pleased?"

The Parable of the Prodigal Son is another story that is often recast to a more relevant setting. There are others as well like The Parable of the Rich Fool and The Parable of the Unjust Steward.

In a later chapter I will talk about giving an Oral Bible and some of the constraints this procedure places on story crafting in the attempt to give a closer-to-verbatim Oral Bible to a people who lack Scriptures in their mother tongue or literacy to read them, so are totally dependent on learned Bible portions.

Chapter 11

Telling the Bible Story

Stories are meant to be told. A dynamic occurs in the live telling of a story in which the story teller and the listeners interact in a world that exists for the duration of the story. In my early years of teaching Bible Storying and going out with some of my trainees to see how they were doing, I accompanied one evangelist who was working among the *Koch* people. We arrived at the village around midmorning. Outside the gate there were people already at work harvesting farm crops. Inside the women were busy with their chores. The evangelist strung up a line on which to hang his Bible pictures. A small crowd of women and children had already begun to gather. The men were out in the fields so this day would be all women. The first picture was hung and the women sat there studying it and waiting to hear the story. A lengthy personal greeting by the storyer and listeners' responses followed. Then the story began.

Across the courtyard an old woman was busy threshing rice with a kind of mortar and pestle device—*chunk, chunk, chunk* as she worked the device, paying no attention to what the other women were doing. But now the story had begun and the chunks were slowing down, slower and slower until the woman stopped. She was obviously listening. Without standing up, the woman began to "duckwalk" across the courtyard until she reached where the other women were sitting on their straw mats. All the while the old woman never took her eyes off the evangelist as he continued his story.

Stories have that power to attract us and draw us into the storytelling community where we become one with the storyteller. Story time is a sharing time. Later we'll discuss the additional sharing in-group before and after the story is told. Now let's look at some of the dynamics of telling your story. It helps if you are a little bit extroverted. If not, don't worry, as you become comfortable telling the stories you will forget any worries about making a mistake or forgetting something important. If you make a mistake your listeners probably won't even notice. Keep focused on the story.

Preparing to Tell Your Stories

Until you can know the stories well enough to be free to tell them without having to refer to your Bible or notes, you will be limited. When you realize that you can open your Bible and then just tell the story it will free you up to give full expression to the story, its plot, and characters.

First, let's look at preparing to tell the story. You must know the story as it is in the Bible. There are different suggestions about how many times to read the story to learn it. I would say not less that three to five readings aloud and ten is better. There is a different way you hear the story when you read it aloud. Sounding the words helps your memory as you get a feel for the story. Then close your Bible and tell the story from what you remember. This procedure provides a good start to a crafted story.

As you read the story, try to see the story happening or sense the story as though you were actually present seeing it happen. Later I will share about fast-tracking longer or extended stories like the Passion Story. To tell this story I must stand in the story and hear the characters speaking, see the action and setting, smell the smells, feel the story, and then tell what I am sensing. You see, by doing this you enter into the story and are no longer recounting an external episode you heard about or read. For you, the story then becomes alive and real, first as you read it, and then later as you tell it. This is an important thing to happen because for oral learners a told story, even one that is about events that happened a long time ago or far away, is for them a current story that is happening right then, right there in their presence. So to tell it, you must sense it, too.

If you are the unusual person you may get the verbatim story well enough to be ready to tell it from memory. But remember, in the earlier chapter on story crafting, I listed a number of things that could make a told story more understandable to listeners who do not know the story. So you will need to think about how to tell the story. You may need the second step of writing the story out as you would like to tell it. Does the story need to be shortened a bit or do some of the many details like some proper names, numbers and geographic names need dropping? Most of us who are literates need to see the story as we write it out.

Remember that you have chosen the story because it addresses some key Bible truths or challenges some world-view issues. Are these clearly addressed in your wording without exaggerating the story? Will the listeners be clear about who is speaking to whom in the story?

It is always good to test your story on a trusted co-worker who will be honest with you if there are any needed changes. Record your story and listen to it. How does it sound? It is easier to record it as you would tell it if you record the story while you are telling it to someone with the same inflections and pauses that you would normally use with your listeners.

There are two opinions about how far ahead to work in preparing Bible stories. One opinion says that it is good to first prepare the whole series of stories so that you are aware of the connections you have made between the earlier and later stories, especially those that are part of a series like the Abraham stories or Exodus stories.

The other opinion suggests that it is only necessary to stay comfortably ahead in story preparation so you can easily make adjustments in future stories as you judge reception and response to stories you are presently telling. Also this second opinion is comforting to those who have developed a long list of stories they believe needed by their listeners. Waiting until the whole series is prepared delays beginning telling the stories.

Either way can work fine. Both have their advantages and disadvantages. However, once a storying strategy has begun and finished you will now have a complete collection of stories along with any corrections and adjustments you made along the way. The most typical changes are additional stories. Occasionally it will be determined that you may drop or hold a story in reserve. David Rodda in his story list uses a 1-4 priority rating from 1 that are "must-tell" stories to 4 which are there if needed.[22] Major attention is given to priority 1 stories.

In your preparation of each story, it is of importance that

you plan to properly relate it to the preceding and following stories. For your listeners this helps to maintain the continuity of the larger story and helps the listeners to carry over important things from one story to the next. Also it helps to preserve the integrity of stories and their relationship to preceding and following stories in a matrix or setting. This may help to prevent faulty interpretation leading to a negative restructuring of individual stories. Some of the story crafting will become intuitive when you begin to tell the stories to your listeners and are able to judge their ability to understand.

One benefit of writing out your stories is that you can share them with others who may lack your skills at story preparation. However, for those who rely solely on someone else's prepared stories, they are robbed of the spiritual growth and personal understanding that comes from studying each story and praying over how to craft it for telling to their listeners.

I started out using someone else's stories and just telling them from their materials. Soon I realized the need to develop my own stories with the crafting and emphasis I needed. Some of the stories those materials used I did not want to use and there were other stories I needed which were not in those materials. In the beginning I was reluctant to share my stories with other missionaries. For one thing the stories were not written down, they existed only orally. But then I realized that I had gained insights that newcomers did not have so they could benefit from my experience.

Also I realized that for some, having a set of already prepared stories, they were more likely to begin telling the stories and would in time move to their own story selection and crafting just as I had done. More story sets or models are being shared as time passes. My only caution is whether this is the best shortcut to take. Some beginning storyers study the prepared stories as models to get ideas for their own story sets. This is better.

Telling Your Bible Stories

Finally the time comes to begin telling the Bible stories you have prepared. We'll talk in the next chapter about the

Storying Session which has several other activities besides telling the Bible stories. Before telling the story you have prepared your listeners by stirring their hearts, provoking their interest in the coming story, and have given them any background information needed to understand the basic story.

Take a deep breath and begin. "Now here is the story from God's Word." Begin telling the story and tell it as a story and not as a report of what happened. You are now the storyteller establishing the setting and circumstances of the story, the one conveying the characters' dialog, and the one commenting as a narrator on what happens in the story just like the Bible writers did.

Professional storytellers say that it is best to "recreate the story" as you tell it, rather than to simply recite it from memory. This is where the tension exists between ability, art, and accuracy. Since a story has life it should be told in a lively manner, preserving that life especially in the dialog between the characters. Dialog slows a story down a bit but makes the story quite personal. Verbs speed the story up and add urgency. Maintain the variety. Use pauses to allow your listeners to follow you and to have a moment to reflect on what is happening. Change tempo where there is action. Change emotional emphasis where there are tension or feeling.

No two people will tell the same story the same way. This is fine. One of my former missionary colleagues in the Philippines said that his wife was the better storyteller. He said that his role was to set up the stories, to develop interest in the story. Then his wife would tell the story. His comment was: "She makes the listeners weep!"

Often I have observed that women are generally better storytellers as they are more likely to be sensitive to the emotions present in the story, and the relationships between characters, and better able to express these creatively. The guys tend to be better at preserving the theological content of the stories and are generally more likely to focus on the setting and action of the plot along with theological undertones.

Let me digress a bit here to deal with several matters

that you may encounter in telling your stories. First, you face the question of whether you use notes to tell your story. Some storyers, after learning their stories and thinking about how to tell them, refer to their open Bibles as they tell the story. Occasionally they will glance at the Bible for a visual cue as they tell the stories basically from memory.

Others who prefer to write out their stories have several choices. Some have used a notebook in which all their stories and learning/teaching activities are listed or outlined. This means not only having an open Bible which is the supposed source of your story, but also another book which you are actually referring to. I faced this dilemma early in my Bible Storying as I held my Bible in one hand and initially a copy of *God and Man* in the other. When I outgrew dependence on the *God and Man* stories, I put my stories on a single piece of paper that I had before me but not as my central focus. I had also used story outline cards attached to the back of teaching pictures that I could see but my listeners could not. One advantage of having a book with all your written stories is that it may facilitate reviewing earlier stories until you learn them well enough to remember them accurately.

Later, especially when using a new story for the first time, I would write out the story word-for-word like I planned to tell it and print is out on my computer as two half-page columns in landscape format. I'd print the story in 14-point type if it would fit on the two pages to make it easy to read. This sheet, folded to fit in my Bible was placed in my Bible so I could refer to it just as I would refer to my Bible pages.

In a few places the listeners have preferred or listened better to a read (recited) story as they knew it was coming from the book and so thought it was more accurate and less likely to be changed. LaNette Thompson reported this among some of her West African women listeners. Another former missionary in Thailand reported that her people listened better to a story from a cassette player as "it always told the story the same way!"

One advantage of using a recorded story is that someone who is fluent in the local language and skilled at telling stories can record the stories. Once recorded, the stories may be used repeatedly without any changes in the way the story is told. What is lost is the dynamic relationship that exists between the storyer who tells the story and the listeners. But a copy of the story may be left behind for the listeners to hear again at their leisure. In the *"Ee-taow!"*[23] story, Mark Zook wore a cassette recorder and recorded all his stories live as he told them. This tape was then available to the *Mouk* people to review on hand-cranked cassette players.

The other matter is that of signaling with the open Bible as you tell the story. What do we mean by "signaling?" This is a sign that the story is coming from the book that you open and hold before you. You have begun with the words, "Now here is the story from God's Word." The opened Bible visualizes this. Early in the Bible Storying experiences I found this helpful to listeners by visualizing this was not my story, but one coming from the book. With some Islamic listeners this has been a critical issue to have this elevating of the Bible as your source from which you are reciting.

The question has been raised by some storyers who felt that opening the Bible placed an object between the storyer and the non-literate listeners. Further, for those sensitive about their lack of literacy it said to them, "I can do something that you cannot do." So the intended good signal was instead a stumbling block.

Several options for working around this are:

- *Open the Bible but leave it on the table or other suitable place while telling the story, but do not hold it or look into it while telling the story.*
- *Hold the Bible up for a moment and then place it on the table as you begin the story.*
- *Only mention that the stories come from a book and you have learned the stories.*
- *Someone told me that, if you really want to be "cool," have someone read or teach the stories to you as you learn them so you can truthfully say, "These are stories I have heard and now I tell them to you."*

At the conclusion of the story, close with the words, "And

that is the end of the story from God's Word." Close the Bible if you have been holding it open and put it down before beginning the discussion activity. If you have not held the Bible, but it is open, close it and place it aside.

With many listeners, especially some high caste Hindus and Sikhs, Buddhist monks, and almost all Muslims, be very careful in your handling of the holy book. Be careful where you place it, not on the ground, nor anything on it. Some storyers find it helpful to have the Bible wrapped in a colorful cloth to be carefully unwrapped and displayed. The little wooden book stands work nicely when with Muslims. I often found it difficult not to hold the Bible in my left (unclean) hand while telling the stories so that I could gesture with my right hand. So in those circumstances leaving the open Bible on a table or stand worked well. As we taught sitting a cushion or bookstand was usually available.

Use a clean copy Bible if it offends your listeners to see that you have written in your Bible. My favorite teaching Bible is one of those chain reference Bibles in which I have added many parallel teaching reference verses in the margins. Once when I was teaching in Bangladesh and my interpreter kept asking for verse references to be sure he was translating correctly, I casually suggested that he should make some notes in his Bible so he wouldn't have to keep asking me. He replied, "Sir, we don't write in our Bibles!"

New Bible storyers often ask whether to stand or sit while telling the stories. The answer depends on personal preferences, circumstances and local culture. My personal preference is to stand so that I can easily gesture, dramatize or be able to walk along a series of pictures if I am reviewing stories. In many circumstances where the storying was conducted in a public place with many listeners, standing was the better option so as to be seen by all. Since I worked with interpreters most of the time we agreed beforehand whether to stand. Among some that I storied the custom was to sit on mats or cushions with the listeners gathered around. One Bengali lady at a training practicum had everyone to sit on the floor while she told her stories. I noticed that many of the pastors that I trained preferred to stand while telling the stories. So from a practical standpoint take your cue first from circumstances, then in consideration of the listeners' culture, and finally personal preferences for teaching. I noticed that many women storyers preferred to sit among their listeners. In Africa the storytellers almost always sat to tell their stories.

When you tell the stories, enjoy the unique relationship you are having with your listeners. At that time you more or less become invisible as the story plays out. There is a sense of community as everyone—storyer and listeners—are engaged in the story at the same time.

What do you do if you forget and leave out something important in the story? I have had to apologize that I made a mistake in telling the story and that I needed to tell it again. I was afraid that I had ruined the story because I made a mistake. But this was redeemed when the listeners said, "That story was so important that you had to tell it correctly."

Don't breathe a sigh of relief just yet. As you will see in the following chapters on the parts of the Bible Storying Session, you may have to tell the story several times. Look at it as additional practice and realize that by doing so you are helping listeners to learn the story so they can recall it with greater accuracy.

Having said all this, let me remind again that the storyer is in a tension between preserving the most accurate account and in facilitating the listeners' hearing, understanding and remembering of the Bible stories. It is a partnership with the Holy Spirit. I always began my stories with a silent prayer before, thanking God for his faithfulness in helping me to tell the stories, and that what I do will be for His honor and glory.

Chapter 12

Storying Session Overview

The concept of an ideal Bible Storying Session came about in several ways. The first influence came in the form of lessons, with discussion questions, teaching comments, and Bible stories modeled in the early story sets shared by New Tribes missionaries in *Chronological Bible Storytelling (54 Bible Stories)*[24] and *God and Man*[25]. These were the Bible story lessons that several of us storying trainers were suggesting for new storyers to use just as we had used them.

Another major influence for me came from many requests by missionaries interested in using Bible Storying but were concerned about what to do and how to fill the time since stories took only a few minutes to tell. Realizing that these proclaimers felt a need for materials drove me to seek to supply the resources.

Storying Session Alternatives for Oral Listeners

In addition was an awareness in my own experience that simply telling a Bible story left the interpretation of the story fairly open to the listeners. I realized that the listeners had not been prepared for the story. Their attention and interest needed focusing on a theme or themes that would help them to understand and apply the story rather than simply interpret it according to their own culture, beliefs, or experiences.

I had also observed that often elaborate greetings would be exchanged before the story session if one of my national co-workers were doing the teaching. Merging out of the greeting was a sharing of recent events among the people. There was an essential need to be sensitive to relationship with the listeners and this was handled in the greeting time. I was reading John D. Wilson's article on "*What it Takes to Reach People in Oral Cultures*" where repetition, context in the form of ritual, and participation were listed as necessary.[26] I comprehended that the Storying Sessions among oral learners were quite relational and, though structured in something like a ritual, had an air of relaxed informality. Time was not an overwhelming factor as long as the listeners were not getting tired from the activities or overloaded with more content than they could mentally process. Once when I was teaching among the *Kek'chi* of Guatemala, I noticed that some of the men stood up as I neared the end of a story I was telling. Then others stood and remained standing. My missionary interpreter whispered in my ear, "They are signaling that it is time to stop!"

There were three obvious parts to a typical storying session. The pre-story time is essential for preparing listeners to hear the stories, to raise their awareness or expectation regarding some truth or happening in the story, and to begin the process of understanding what the story teaches them. Next, telling the story is the central event that is important in its own right. The post-story time is needed to review, guide, and facilitate listeners to appropriate the truths in the stories and apply them to their lives. Sometimes I use the expression "a time for them to begin digesting the story and its implication for them."

To incorporate John Wilson's suggestions I began to experiment with my own story groups. Out of the various activities that I tried there evolved a list of pre-story activities which for convenience sake storying trainers call the *Pre-story Dialog*. Following the Bible story another set of post-story activities helped the storyer guide and facilitate the learning that was taking place. The trainers called this action the *Post-story Dialog*.

The term *dialog* was used deliberately to encourage listener participation as opposed to *monolog* or lecture teaching. It has been pointed out that oral learners learned best when they discovered things on their own rather than being told directly what they should believe. The dialog approach encourages the needed participation which in my experience definitely fosters learning by the listeners. We'll come back to this and illustrate it as an important concept. It is difficult for some to accept the possibility of dialog when they believe that a teacher with knowledge should "teach" in order to cause listeners to "learn" so that neither truth in the story nor any implication is missed by the listeners. Notice that I used the expression "learning/teaching" which puts an emphasis on their learning at their pace with teaching largely guiding their learning and answering their questions.

To illustrate the issue of self-discovery versus being told what to believe, let me share an anecdote told by Walter J. Ong regarding a Russian researcher named Luria.

> In the Far North, where there is snow, all bears are white. Novaya Zembla is in the Far North and there is always snow there. What color are the bears?" Here is the typical response, "I don't know. I've seen a black bear. I've never seen any others....Each locality has its own animals"...When the syllogism was given to him a second time, a barely literate 45-year-old chairman of a collective farm manages, "To go by your words, they should all be white.[27]

I was teaching the Bible stories among the *Kui* of India. After the stories of the Creation of Man, the Flood, the repopulation of the earth, and the Tower of Babel, an elderly man spoke to me through my interpreter: "I am hearing in these stories that Noah is my grandfather. Is that true?" I agreed that it was. He continued, "Is Noah your grandfather also?" I agreed that was so. Then he replied, "If Noah is my grandfather and if Noah is your grandfather, then we are brothers! That is good news. I am like you!" The man reasoned out the stories and the implication for him. A missionary storyer in South America reported this response, "After reviewing the OT stories one of the I... leaders said with eyes wide open: 'I believe we have sinned.'" Another man in a different country confessed, "We are FRIED! What chance do we have?" Now that was self-discovery! Later it was reported the man and his family became believers after hearing the stories of Jesus and were baptized.

The implication for telling Bible stories to those hostile to traditional teaching also points to the need for self-discovery. Among Muslims to state that Jesus is the Son of God will most likely end the friendly conversation. But, if the stories that are told illustrate the characteristics of Jesus being like those of the Father, and the words of the characters in the stories confess in testimony that Jesus is God's Son, then it is much more likely for listeners to come to that self-discovery than to be told it is so. All listeners may need is a review and reflection time to think about these things following the stories to decide for themselves.

Other terms have also been used to define the learning times. One term I often use is *Discovery Time*, especially for the period following the Bible story when it is discussed. In one set of model story lessons I did for women I used the terms "Open the Women's Minds" for the Pre-Story Dialog and "Open the Women's Hearts" for the Post-Story Dialog. The idea being to get the women started thinking in a certain direction and then after the story to get them to open their hearts to discover the truths in the stories.

When the first requests came for help in knowing what to do before and after telling a story I had suggested preparing the listeners and then helping the listeners to draw meaning and understanding from the stories. I was doing these things intuitively without really thinking in terms of defined lesson activities. But those who were asking for help wanted structure — defined and written out steps, resources or activities which could be used to help in planning their teaching and directing the learning/teaching when the stories were told. Response to these requests led to the sets of learning activities that I will discuss in the next two chapters on the Pre-Story Dialog and the Post-Story Dialog.

It is my opinion that the Bible story is the most important aspect of a storying session. It is the focal point. There is even a training motto: "If you can't do anything else, at least tell the story!" All that is done before the story is told should prepare listeners by connecting the present story to earlier stories, and point to the new story, and the truths it conveys or worldview issues it challenges for which the story was selected. Following the story all that is done should serve to reinforce remembering the story and lead from the story and its truths to listeners' hearts and application in their lives.

Over time some interesting things have been observed regarding the Storying Sessions. The sessions have not worked equally well everywhere. For one thing the suggested activities work best if the group is relatively small—probably less than 20-30 listeners. As the size of the group grows the activities become more rhetorical than participative and tend to be more proclamation than individual or group discovery. Among non-literate storyers their sessions tended to be very simple with little teaching outside of telling the story and asking simple questions to review the story points and make application. Some literate pastors preferred to tell the stories and comment on them much like a sermon.

Among some peoples in the Orient there is a fear of losing face if one does not possess the correct answer. So this leads to a reticence to respond out of a fear of being shamed. Out of respect for the teacher others become ashamed if they do not know the correct answer. For they believe this casts shame upon the teacher for not teaching them well.

In one instance from Africa it was said that a group of women, upon hearing the stories and being asked questions regarding the stories, remained silent until one of the women volunteered, "We don't know. No one has ever asked our opinion before." A note was added: The women soon lost their timidity and were caught up in the stories which provoked their lively discussion. LaNette Thompson in her diary of their first story sessions in Burkina Faso told of the presence of a *delegué* among the men who was the designated spokesman for the men. When asking questions of the group it was the *delegué* who replied. When he was absent the men could respond personally.[28]

However, among many of the people groups that I taught where the group was small, the response to the stories warmed up as the people grew to know me and as the listeners learned to "play the game." In learning activities that are repetitive there is comfort for oral learners in knowing the system or ritual that becomes routine after several sessions. This usually promotes openness and sharing over time. In the Thai culture this makes learning "*sanuk*" or fun.

In a story set for Muslim women I did not include any suggested pre- or post-story activities or discussion as the problem was that some women did not want any "Christian" teaching but were interested in the stories about women. However, the Bible stories about women who suffered misfortune provoked much response by the listeners with many questions and group discussion as the stories continued. So the patient storyer would finally get to provide at the women's request the very thing the women initially said they did not want.

In a later chapter I will mention some of the common problems that have arisen related to the Storying Sessions. One in particular has been that of children taking over the responses, allowing the adults to remain silent. From the Bible storyer's perspective there is need for flexibility in developing sessions that are productive and interesting for the listeners rather than slavishly following a set of steps or activities that are on a list. In fact it is important for the Storying Sessions to have a seamless flow so the listeners are less aware of moving from activity to activity.

The following two chapters then are provided as resources to give ideas about learning activities that are participative, repetitive, and structured to aid the learning/teaching process during the Storying Sessions. Again let me stress, these are resources to utilize as appropriate and needed, and not rules to follow. This structure will aid the storyer in preparing for their Storying Sessions by giving discrete activities which can be prepared in advance and used as needed.

Storying Session Alternatives for Literate Listeners

It is important to note that the ideal storying session has resources primarily for the oral learner. As the degree of literacy increases there are other options for leading an interesting and rewarding learning/teaching session. Among literates the participation may be in the form of their taking turns reading from the stories in their Bibles, studying maps and timeline charts, watching videos or viewing other projected helps via equipment likely to be available in urban storying situations. In addition, study notes can be given out and reading assignments made to prepare for future Storying Sessions.

Telling Bible stories still adds a dimension to the stories by the added emphases of the narrator and the fact that the listeners are receiving the story as a group and responding as a group which adds a dynamic all its own. Pre-Story and

Post-Story Dialog is still a fine idea to prepare the literate listeners as well as to give a time following the story to discuss implications. One activity that has worked well among younger literate listeners is to give listening tasks. After the story, divide listeners up into discussion or buzz groups which then report back to the gathered group. Because the listeners are literate, and if they possess or have access to a Bible or Scripture portions, then various related Scriptures can be looked up to enrich the teaching and as a way of answering questions that arise regarding the story.

Where several different Bible versions exist among literate listeners it might be helpful to provide handouts with the story passage and any reference verses so that all will be able to follow and not get involved in discussion about why one version says one thing and another something different. If a written story lesson is used, some storyers prefer not giving out the printed materials until after the story is told.

Literate listeners should still enjoy retelling the stories just as their oral counterparts. It is not uncommon for there to be some initial hesitation if literates are not used to remembering and sharing orally. But once the ice is broken most will enjoy the experience. The main difference is that some literates may want to memorize the stories versus creatively retelling the story in their own words.

One thing to remember with oral learners is the fact that they tire easily in lengthy exercises. Unless oral learners are accustomed to responding to catechisms or answering questions which require reflection, fatigue can come quickly. When the learning/teaching exercises are completed it is good to stop and have some fellowship with the listeners. This can be very important if the story and Dialog time challenge their spiritual beliefs or lifestyles. It is a way of maintaining the relationship outside of the teaching session.

Chapter 13
Pre-Story Dialog Time

The Pre-Story Dialog time is very important as it provides the connecting point between the storyer and listeners and between the new story and previous stories. In addition this dialog develops the initial focus for the new story and its truths. The following learning/teaching activities reinforce these connections and begin developing the needed focus for the Bible story to follow.

Once again the storyer should remember that these are suggested resources that can be used in part or whole as needed. The list is only descriptive as each storyer will develop a Storying Session that meets the needs of his/her listeners.

Typical Pre-Story Dialog learning/teaching activities are:

- *Begin with a culturally appropriate greeting.*
- *Ask about recent happenings to get listeners engaged and talking, showing your concern about them.*
- *Continue with a recall/review of recent stories.*
- *Recall core Bible stories, especially those needed as background for the new story.*
- *Encourage listeners to ask questions about previous stories.*
- *Begin building anticipation by asking exploratory (sensitizing) questions related to the theme or truths in the new story.*
- *Bridge or link previous stories to the current story.*
- *Tell an entry or bridging story that leads into main story.*
- *Give a Listening Task.*

These activities pick up the listeners where they are in their lives and bring them to the story. Remember this is primarily talking about oral learners who largely live in rural communal environments in cultures that are highly relational. The activities are structured to foster the relationship between the storyer as an outsider and the group. It does this by increasingly involving the listeners in participation as illustrated in the following:

Culturally appropriate greeting to establish relationship and demonstrate concern beyond the storying task

One thing that task-oriented Westerners need to remember is that a proper relationship is quite important in most oral communities. The storyer has come from the outside after a period of time and now re-enters the communal fellowship.

I remember well something I was told years ago when I was itching to get started with the storying session. My Bengali host said to me, "Fust (*sic*) we take tea!" After tea and some visiting he indicated that now it was time to get started. The greeting often serves another purpose in that it allows the storyer to recognize the leaders and pay due respects to the elders among the listeners. Generally this is with the men only when a man is leading the storying or a woman when storying to a women's group. Political and religious leaders are often offended if greeting is not done in a socially acceptable manner.

Ask about recent happenings which might reveal what is on the hearts and minds of listeners

Knowledge of recent events may be helpful in relating the new story to the listeners. Knowledge of these events can in some circumstances prevent untimely remarks or even the use of stories at a sensitive time for listeners. These events can also have a positive effect by opening the listeners' hearts for a word of comfort or hope.

How long to allot to this and when to stop is something that the storyer will need to sense. If the storyer is not going to touch on truths related to any recent events on that day, it does provide information for pointing to future stories and for the storyer to incorporate appropriate dialog items into future learning/teaching activities. LaNette Thompson related in her *Diaradugu Diary*[29] information about the time she and her husband arrived and found that the chief of that larger area had died and the village was officially in mourning. So they did not story that day but went to the home of the local village chief who was sick to pay their respects.[30]

Recall and review core stories or those needed as background or introductory stories for the current story

Now the opportunity is given for listeners to retell previous stories. The storyer might ask, "Who can tell last week's story?" Or, "Who can tell the story of....?" First of all this retelling is a form of review as the listeners hear the stories told anew. Also it is a review as the main or core stories are reviewed. How far back to review? That depends. If the new story is on God's judgment, then several previous stories that illustrated God's judgment would be in order. This review also tells the storyer how well the stories are holding up—are they being altered in some way? Are the stories fading from their memory? Do listeners need to hear the storyer tell the stories again to refresh their memory? As the listeners volunteer to retell stories, if they stumble, it may be appropriate to ask if another would help them to continue. They may do this automatically as part of the story accuracy depends on the group memory. If the retelling is a poor one, then thank the person and ask if someone else would like to tell the story. I like to use the expression "keep fishing" until you get a good retelling. If not, then you the storyer will retell it. So that means the storyer must keep the stories in mind as well.

Allow listeners to ask questions about previous stories

This is very important to do. True, the storyer is the teacher. But remember, the objective is to encourage learning. And if something has lingered heavy on listeners' hearts and they want to ask about it, this is good to know. If the storyer senses hostility, he/she should answer with a question referring to earlier stories or simply let the person express their view. This is not the place to get into a debate. Generally the objective is to keep the storying session "win/win" so the people will keep listening.

Questions relate to several areas of importance. Some questions arise out of the listeners' lack of a frame of reference for something in a previous story — something that doesn't make sense to them or that is strange to their culture and they don't know what to think about the matter. The second area has to do with issues that challenge their spiritual worldview and they want to talk about it or even express an opinion. In the *"Ee-taow!"*[31] video, an older man is bothered by what Abraham is going to do since God has asked him to sacrifice his son. So the man sought out Mark Zook to say that he knew God would somehow provide a way to save Isaac. It is good to know that stories have stirred hearts and the listeners are still thinking about the stories.

Begin building anticipation by asking exploratory questions which pose the problems or issues the new story will include or address.

These may be rhetorical questions asked simply to stir up thinking and sensitize listeners to the theme or a particular truth in the story. The questions can be used to provoke free discussion in which there are no right or wrong answers. Listen for clues to their beliefs or lack of understanding in their answers. I have always said that if you get a good conversational buzz going among the listeners that is good. You have not lost control, but have stirred their thinking.

How many questions are needed? Usually only a few are all that is required. In the *God and Woman* model preceding the story of the birth of Isaac's sons, I asked some women about what happens when a woman is barren? And I followed that with a question about who can take away the disgrace? In another lesson I asked if anyone in the group had ever been betrayed by another. Apparently some had. I got the desired "buzz" from the women and they were ready to hear what happened in the coming story. The listeners' responses may be surprising and are often a good source for understanding their worldviews. The more you know about their worldview and everyday life, the more relevant the questions can be to spark interest and response.

Begin bridging or linking previous stories to the current story

This is very important with some like Muslims, especially if the coming story challenges existing beliefs. One thing in the favor of the Bible storyer is that the Bible stories are related and coherently linked by various threads that tie them together. Tracing these threads may be characters who continue through several stories, genealogical threads like at the end of the Ruth story that link it to the story of David, promises of God (like God made to Abraham, Isaac and Jacob), or threatened judgment as found in the stories of the kingdoms and prophets, and other themes which carry over from story to story. The integrity of the Bible account is maintained.

One of the characteristics of folk stories common among listeners is that stories may exist that are not consistent or that outright contradict one another. This is generally not a problem as these are "just stories." In the Quran beginning in surah 11:2 and following is the story of Noah's son who was among those who drowned but later God raised back to life. There are many other errors as those story fragments are not logically connected and related, lacking overall narrative integrity.

If necessary, tell a linking story—a compressed story that has a basic purpose to set a frame of reference for the current story or relate it to earlier core stories. The previous activity was that of reviewing links to earlier stories. Now is the time to tell a story that leads into the main story of the day. It is not the purpose of this linking story to supply many details but merely to provide an introduction. Let me illustrate.

In my early days of storying when I told the story of David and Bathsheba, I soon realized that this story was not at all considered wrongdoing by the listeners. David was the king and as king could do pretty much as he chose. So I was led to the story of David and his mighty men bodyguards in 2 Samuel 23 in which the incident of David's longing for a drink of water from the well at Bethlehem (his home) led to three of the men getting the water for David. But he would not drink it because that water was gotten at risk of his men's lives—it represented their blood. There are several brief anecdotes of the exploits of the bodyguards and then a list of thirty-seven that includes Bathsheba's husband Uriah and her father Eliam (see 2Sam. 11:3). Now there was a social relationship and violating that is not good. The purpose of this story is not to tell about the bodyguards but to give a good reference frame or establish relationship between David, Uriah, and Bathsheba's family for the main story. Usually these introductory stories are paraphrased or compressed into a basic story using only the essential details.

Give a Listening Task if that is appropriate

Listening Tasks are helpful for inviting participation of the listeners to watch for something in the main story and then to tell what they found. This may be likened to giving an opportunity for listeners to "play the game". In the *God and Man* model story set, the Schultzes used a chart of the Characteristics of God to prepare the listeners for a listening task in the story.[32] The task was "Listen to this story and see how many of the characteristics of God you can find." When I had used the story of Naboth's Vineyard I liked to review the Ten Commandments with my listeners. I said the Ten Commandments several times and had the listeners to repeat the Ten Commandments so they were fresh in listeners' memories. Then I said to the listeners, "Now listen to this story about a man named Naboth and see how many of God's Commandments were broken."

Questions about what the listeners found in the story usually provoke a lively discussion. The Listening Task helps to give an additional focus to the story, keep the listeners alert, and give opportunity to participate. One other comment I will make is that use of Listening Tasks can help to tie Old and New Testament stories together. There is a slightly different set of *Characteristics of Allah* that I use for Muslims that I have the listeners look for in the Old Testament stories. Then in the Gospel stories they are to look for the characteristics that Jesus had that were like those of Allah. It is a subtle precursor of relating Jesus to the Father.

If any of these activities are not appropriate, especially those involving the listeners' participation, then use discretion about whether to use them or not. If the storyer has some additional ideas for learning/teaching activities that help recalling and reviewing as well as provoking expectation and anticipation in the Bible story, then by all means consider using them.

Remember that the Pre-Story Dialog time primarily is to prepare the listeners for the new story. So do not overload them with large amounts of detail or explanation. Review of earlier stories is very important as the chronological progression continues to keep a sense of continuity and development, and also to refresh the earlier stories. A balance of participation in having listeners recall the stories and sensitizing dialog to stir up curiosity is needed. Part of the art of Bible Storying is sensing when your listeners are ready for the new story. However, if they are not properly prepared they may fail to see the connection or relationship to earlier stories or, worse yet, to understand the new story because they lack some key bit of information needed to appreciate it or to relate to it. In time and practice the Pre-Story Dialog time becomes easier to prepare and lead.

Chapter 14

Post-Story Dialog Time

The Post-Story Dialog is second in importance only to the Bible story itself. The term "dialog" is crucial during this time as this discussion is meant to be a discovery time which requires a participatory dialog with oral learners for best results. Just as in the Pre-Story Dialog this practice includes review and interactive times. I will supply the resource list of activities along with several options for leading a Post-Story Dialog time. These options provide approaches which are quite different.

First, I direct your attention to the typical Post-Story Dialog resources. Second, I will present several strategy options for leading a Post-Story Dialog.

Learning Activities for Post-Story Dialog Sessions

Seven resources aid in the post-dialog sessions:

- *Immediate retelling of the new story by listeners.*
- *Responses to the Listening Task if used.*
- *Simple questions to review the facts in the stories.*
- *Probing questions to reveal if the listeners understood the story and its implications for them.*
- *Drama or role play if needed to visualize the story.*
- *Dialog about what the listeners should think, believe, or do now that they have heard the story.*
- *Memory verse practice (related to the story).*

Immediate Retelling of the New Story

It is important to get an immediate feedback on how the listeners heard the story and what they might change in their retelling. Just as during the review of stories in the Pre-Story Dialog, it is helpful to keep asking for someone to retell the story until a good retelling is achieved.

If an adequate retelling is not achieved, then the storyer will say something like this: "Perhaps you did not hear the story well. Let me tell it again for you." An alternative to having individuals retell long stories is to have someone begin the story and go as far as they can, then another pick up the story with some prompting if required, until the story is told. This requires patience on the part of the storyer. The group of oral learners will not mind hearing the story again and again.

Get Responses to the Listening Task if Used

Repeat the Listening Task and then call for volunteers to respond. Again, it may take some probing to get a correct answer. In my experience using the Characteristics of God chart or looking for breaking the Ten Commandments as the Listening Task, the listeners are not too discriminating in the beginning. Some will say they found all of the items whether actually in the story or not. Again, have patience as the listeners get better at this activity and in time will begin self-correcting when someone gives the wrong answer. If working with students or those with a degree of literacy and greater exposure to buzz groups, it is helpful to let small groups work on the Listening Task as well as some of the review questions, and then report back to the larger group.

Ask Simple Questions to Review the Basic Facts of the Story

This is to be sure the listeners have understood the story well enough to ferret out the characters, perhaps where the story takes place, and the basic plot. There may also be some portion of the dialog between characters that is important to remember. In this activity do not ask for opinions, only facts.

One issue that can come up is that many oral learners could be slow to pick these things out of the story. For some the story is a whole and is understood as a whole without real awareness of component parts. Younger people will usually be better at picking out these details. Be patient.

Ask Probing Questions to Test Understanding and Implication

It is quite important that listeners not be allowed to hold a story at arm's length, so to speak. The idea is to get the listeners to internalize the story, to see a relationship to it, to find themselves in the story. I have used various methods to do this. One has been to ask various listeners what they would do if they were one of the characters in the story. Or I would ask if any of the listeners were like any of the characters in the story? Or has anything like the story happened to any of the listeners?

There are many ways that questions can be asked. Some storyers merge the factual questions right on into the relational questions and then on to the application questions. Oral learners get tired quickly when pressed with many questions. There are storying models that may use as many as twenty questions that require factual answers or to give opinions. If the most important questions are pushed too far down the list, listeners may tire before reaching the important relational and applicational questions. Experience with a group will help to judge when this is happening.

Use Drama or Role Play to Visualize Story

Anything that can be done to visualize the story will generally help understanding and remembering the story. This is participative play that is relaxing for the listeners and allows them to "try on" various character roles in the story which may be role play or drama with dialog. The listeners themselves or a mix of storyer team and listeners may enact the drama.

I have participated in several dramas. Once I was one of the people who died in the Flood. At another time I was part of the multitude that Jesus fed. However, one of my favorite times was once when telling the story of Elijah on Mt. Carmel I performed a little jig while shouting "Oh, Baal, hear us!" to illustrate the frustration of the false prophets. The listeners loved it and in that place would ask me to tell that story each time I visited.

Actually I made it a practice later to do gesturing and simple drama movement, as I told the stories. Fortunately I had interpreters most of the time who would work with me.

Be prepared for extraneous things to be introduced into some dramas. Once when the listeners were performing the story of the Prodigal Son the pigs were behaving in such a way that listeners were laughing. I feared that the story was being turned into a travesty. But then the son saw his father standing in the distance waiting and got up to run to his father and fall before him to confess his sin. The laughter of a minute before was now tears at this touching scene.

Dialog About Listener Response to Story

At this point in the storying process the net is drawn for the individual story. It is the application of the story truths to the listeners' lives. Some stories mainly provide information so this would relate to beliefs. Other stories provide warnings or encouragement and so provide clues about what not to do and what one should do. The ideal would be for the listeners to say something like, "If this story is true, then we should…." In other words it is hoped they see for themselves what the story should mean to them or teach them to do.

Give a Memory Verse

Initially I did not use memory verses following the stories but later realized this is not only another participative activity but a fine way to encapsulate the story in a verse that captures its teaching or meaning. In addition many of the verses begin to form an important source of Scripture for worship when that day comes. The drill is to quote the verse several times, then have the listeners quote it with you, and finally to have individual listeners to quote the verse. Other verses can be quoted in review. Just remember that the storyer must remember these as well! These verses form an important meditation resource for encouraging an oral daily quiet time.

Options for Conducting Post-Story Dialog

Having covered these possible activities as resources, now consider several different options for conducting the Post-Story Dialog:

Open or Free Discussion Following the Story

This activity has been a favorite of mine for several reasons. I have worked among people groups who were very responsive and so on their own would begin responding to the Bible story. Sometime the discussion would be started by simply asking, "What did you hear? Let's talk about it." Someone might ask a question related to the story and I would respond with another question that pointed toward an answer or that opened up still other questions or observations. We talked until the group was satisfied or tired!

This approach worked best when training pastors and other emerging leaders. But it also worked well in small groups where we sat around and informally talked and shared. One advantage is that often the direction of discussion would help me to understand how the group was hearing the story, and many times would reveal things in the stories that I missed or was insensitive to because of my culture. The disadvantage is that some important issues could be missed in the story unless the group were prodded to keep them on track.

Resource Model With Various Learning/Teaching Activities

This model provides a middle ground in that it is a guided discussion time but has a variety to it that breaks it up into smaller activities to keep it interesting. The number of discussion questions is usually limited to only four to five main questions of facts and internalizing, and perhaps only one or two application questions. The storyer develops the questions related to each story as part of the preparation.

One of the disadvantages when teaching the storying model to oral leaders for their use is that it is too complicated for them to remember all the different questions for each story. So this is basically a missionary storyer's discussion model.

A Structured Model

A third model is a structured factual Q & A that makes use of many questions that explore the facts of the story, the truths taught by the story, even questions that relate the present story to previous stories, and questions that may call for opinions or value judgments. I sometimes refer to this as an exhaustive discussion—it exhausts the subject and the listeners! But it is thorough and can work well for some storyers and listeners who can handle the list of questions without tiring. One storyer indicated that she used this approach to strictly control the discussion because of language limitations and to prevent getting into hostile debate.

Limited Set of Exploration Questions

A Post-Story Dialog model that is more reproducible makes use of a limited set of exploration questions which are used for all the stories. Once the list of questions is learned it can be used over and over by oral leaders as they tell the stories. There are several versions of which I am aware of. One comes from Ethiopia and another comes from Bangladesh. Both are listed in the "Bible Storying Helps".

Conclusion

In review, the purpose of the Post-Story Dialog is to facilitate the listeners as they process the Bible story and find ways to relate to it and apply it to their lives. The Dialog is generally guided by the storyer in a kind of inductive study that is culturally appropriate and manageable by the listeners according to their educational and experience levels. It is possible for the early stories to have simpler Dialogs and for these to grow more exhaustive toward the end of the story track.

For those who are telling the stories to literates and those with more educational experience, there are additional options. One is a deductive lecture option in which the story is told and then an interpretive investigative monolog teaching follows. This approach also allows for questions and additional discussion according to the interest and needs of the listeners. Study sheets may be used that contain the story if it is crafted significantly different from the Bible text, and a study outline or questions for individual study.

Avoid getting trapped into debates. When questions are asked, respond with a question if it is sensed that a debate is likely to follow. When questions are asked or issues brought up that have not yet been covered by stories or discussion, then defer to later stories and make a note to point out the answers then. It is good to keep the focus on the Bible and use the Bible to interpret the Bible as much as possible. Remember that listeners who are learning the stories so they can retell them to others will not have all the knowledge that the missionary storyer has.

When storying to large groups it is obvious that attempting to initiate all the possible learning/teaching activities is difficult if not impossible. In those cases I told the stories and then reviewed several key points using rhetorical questions, or quoted additional Scripture passages or reviewed previous stories. I suspect that my interpreters were doing a bit of preaching on their own!

If more than one major story is told, then the Post-Story Dialog gets complicated and for this reason it is recommended that only one major story or at most a cluster of smaller stories with a common theme be used at any one Storying Session. This procedure prevents overload of oral learners when all stories are dissected and explored.

Chapter 15

Model Bible Story Session

This Model Bible Storying Session is typical of how I might plan a session or share my session plans with another storyer. Some of the activities require listener participation so they are just listed. While I have a session plan, I know to remain flexible and ready to vary it if I sense a need to change. After the first few stories it becomes easier to read your listeners and predict how they will respond to the session and the optimum length for a session. There are always surprises. LaNette Thompson related in her *Diaradugu Diary* how on one occasion that she and her husband Marvin arrived and...

> "Upon arrival no one was present at the 'storytelling tree.' A wedding was underway in a nearby courtyard and the entire village was involved. A group of men came striding over. 'Let's get started right away,' they said. 'Don't waste any time because we want to get back to the wedding.' Eventually 24 men gathered. A woman went to call the women who were involved in the food preparation and 15 came. A terrible dust storm arose and swirled about us. We had to shout to be heard. The people still sat, huddled under *pagnas*, listening eagerly."[33]

I was meeting with a listener group in western Bangladesh just at the start of the monsoon season when the planting rains came. The men came from their plowing in the fields to listen. Storm clouds were gathering to the northwest from where the monsoons came. The listeners were becoming very agitated. Finally one of the men urged us to hurry up as the rains were coming and they needed to finish their plowing. So we honored their request and cut short the session after telling the story. Plan to be flexible!

Many story sets in the early days were not written sets, but were simply agreed upon oral story sets. When missionaries began requesting lists of the stories, they wanted to know how to tell certain stories and for help with worldview issues. It became helpful to write out the story sets as models to share. All of the early written models in the areas where I worked were in English. Later many of these models were either translated or used as a basis for developing local language models for sharing with both missionaries and literate workers.

Here then is one model story from a set that we have used. Storyers can use this model as an illustration for any Bible story that they think is needed by the group they serve.

The Suffering Servant

(*name of story set*)

JESUS HAD NO PLACE TO CALL HIS HOME (*lesson title*)

Scriptures to Study: Isa. 53:3; Mt. 4:18-21; 8:19-22; Mk. 3:20-35; 8:34-38; Lk. 4:14-30; Jn. 1:11; 7:2-9.

Talk About These Things: (*pre-story dialog*)

1. What would cause you to dislike a person? Their appearance? Their family or background? Their teaching?
2. Have you ever had to leave home and continue to move about without a home which you could return to?
3. Would you follow someone who moved about continually teaching and healing?
4. Which is more important to you—obeying God or having a comfortable life at home?

Read From Bible: Mt. 8:19-22; Lk. 4:28-30

Tell the Story:

Jesus Had No Place to Call His Home

After Jesus was baptized by John and tempted by Satan, he returned to his own home town of Nazareth. When the day of worship came Jesus went to the worship hall to pray. He was asked to read from the Holy Scriptures and teach from them. The attendant gave Jesus a scroll of the Prophet Isaiah. And Jesus read these words:

"The Spirit of the Lord is on me, because he has anointed me to preach good news to the poor. He has sent me to

> proclaim freedom to the prisoners and recovery of sight for the blind, to release the oppressed, to proclaim the year of the Lord's favor." When he had finished reading, Jesus rolled up the scroll and gave it back to the attendant and sat down to teach (Luke 4:18-20).

The eyes of everyone in the worship hall were fixed on Jesus. He said to them, "Today this scripture has been fulfilled in your hearing." All those present spoke well of Jesus and were amazed at the gracious words that came from his lips. "Isn't this the son of Joseph the carpenter?" they asked. Then Jesus said, "Surely you will quote to me this proverb: 'Physician, heal yourself! Do here in your home town what we have heard you did in other places.' But I tell you the truth," Jesus continued, "no prophet is accepted in his home town." Then Jesus told two stories about how the prophets of old had helped or healed those who were not descendants of Abraham, but were foreigners.

When the people heard these stories and words of Jesus they were furious. They got up, seized Jesus, and drove him out of the town, intending to throw him down from a cliff on the side of the hill where the town stood. But Jesus walked right through the crowd and went his way.

Jesus had called men to follow him. As he was walking beside the Sea of Galilee he saw two brothers who were fishermen casting their nets into the water. He said to Simon and Andrew, "Follow me, and I will make you fishers of men." They left their nets and followed Jesus. Then he saw another two brothers, James and John, preparing their nets. He called them and immediately they left their boat and their father and followed Jesus. And still another named Matthew was a tax collector. As Matthew was sitting at his booth collecting tax money Jesus said, "Follow me," and immediately Matthew left his tax booth and followed Jesus. In all there were twelve men that Jesus called to be his disciples—men with whom he would teach and travel.

One day when a crowd had gathered around Jesus, a teacher of the law came to him and said, "Teacher, I will follow you wherever you go." Jesus replied, "Foxes have holes and birds of the air have nests, but the Son of Man has no place to lay his head."

Even Jesus' own family had rejected him. One day when Jesus had entered a house and a crowd gathered, he began to teach them. When Jesus' family heard about this, they went to take charge of him for they said, "He is out of his mind." Some of the teachers of the law were there also accusing Jesus of being possessed by the devil saying, "He has an evil spirit." Jesus rebuked them with a parable saying, "A kingdom cannot be divided against itself or it will not stand. How can Satan drive out Satan? No one can enter a strong man's house and rob him unless he first binds the strong man."

Then Jesus' mother and brothers arrived. Standing outside, they sent someone in to call Jesus. They told him, "Your mother and brothers are looking for you." Then Jesus looked at the crowd seated all about him in a circle and said, "Here are my mother and my brothers! Whoever does God's will is my brother and sister and mother."

At another time Jesus told the crowd and his disciples: "If anyone would come after me, he must deny himself and take up his cross and follow me. For whoever wants to save his life will lose it, but whoever loses his life for my sake and for the Good News will save it."

When time came for one of the feasts in Jerusalem, Jesus' brothers came to him and said, "You ought to leave this place and go to Jerusalem, so that your disciples may see the miracles you do. No one who wants to become a public figure acts in secret. Since you are doing these things, go show yourself to the world!" Jesus' brothers said these things because they did not believe in him.

One of the disciples named John later wrote: "He came to those who were his own, but his own did not receive him. Yet to all who received him, to those who believed in his name, he gave the right to become the children of God—children born not of natural descent...but born of God." (NIV)

Let's Talk Some More: (*post-story dialog*)

1. Where had Jesus gone on the day of worship? (*To the worship hall to pray*)
2. What did the leader ask him to do? (To read from the Holy Scriptures and give a teaching)

3. Did the people like the teaching of Jesus? (Yes, in the beginning. But they did not like what Jesus began to teach about how God loved and helped all people.)
4. What did Jesus say about a prophet and the prophet's own people? (*He was not accepted by his own people.*) Do you remember a prophecy that said the promised Anointed One would be rejected by his own people? (*Read again Isa. 53:3*)
5. When Jesus called certain men to follow him what did they do? (*They left their work and began to follow Jesus.*) Do you think they really knew who Jesus was? (*Most likely not*)
6. Do you think the teacher of the law was sincere when he said he would follow Jesus? (Probably. But Jesus warned him that it would not be easy since Jesus had no home to call his own.)
7. Again when Jesus was teaching the people who had gathered around him and some were accusing Jesus of being demon-possessed, what did Jesus' family want to do? (*They thought he was out of his mind. They went to get him and bring him home.*) What do you think Jesus meant when he said that the people sitting around him who do God's will are his family?
8. What do you think Jesus meant that if anyone would follow him, they must deny themselves and take up their crosses and follow Jesus? (**Note:** *Don't explain this now. Let the group talk about it.*)
9. When Jesus' own brothers came to him to urge him to go to Jerusalem and proclaim who he was, do you think they were sincere? (*No. They were mocking Jesus because they did not believe in him at that time.*) Do you think these words and the earlier words of his family when they came to get him caused Jesus to suffer?
10. We didn't talk about it in this story but there were people who cared about Jesus. Some of the wealthy women gave money to meet his needs. (*Lk. 8:2-3*) Two women and their brother Lazarus were friends. Jesus visited their home with his disciples to rest and to eat. (*Lk. 10:38-42*) Later we will have a story about a guest room a man

allowed Jesus to use for eating the Passover Feast with his disciples. And there is another story about a man who gave his tomb for Jesus to use. Jesus had no home but he had many friends who helped him.

A Verse to Remember: *"He came to that which was his own, but his own did not receive him. Yet to all who received him, to those who believed in his name, he gave the right to become children of God." Jn. 1:11*[34]

There are many things in this Storying Session that relate to the Bengali worldview. The Bengali people see themselves as a suffering people and can identify with one who suffers. The typical rural people have little beyond their simple houses, cooking and farm utensils and a change of clothes. Many are fishermen and can identify with the disciples whom Jesus called. In communal societies the parts of the story about Jesus and the worshipers who rejected him and the event when his family came to get him would make sense. This particular story is a bit atypical in that it is a longer narrative that consists of several short accounts. But it demonstrates how the Pre-Story Dialog leads into the story and the Post-Story Dialog then helps to facilitate the processing of the story by listeners.

The review of earlier stories and call for retelling the new story were not listed in the model as these things are part of the basic storying methodology and would be done automatically at each session.

Chapter 16

Drawing the Net

Bringing Closure to the Evangelism Track

Early Responders

There is the possibility for some listeners being ready to believe in Jesus before the end of the Bible story Evangelism Track. Some of the listeners may already be *cultural Christians* having previous knowledge of the Bible and Jesus. Perhaps they may be clamoring to begin having "church." This was true in the Philippines where some of the lowland cultural Christians lived among the tribal groups. And it was also true in India where many had already been exposed to Christianity during a hospital stay or relief project. Depending upon what they have previously heard or experienced, the Bible teaching, even before reaching the stories of Jesus, can trigger a salvation desire. If so, take the listeners aside privately, as opportunity permits, and question them. Do they understand who Jesus is and why God sent him? Do they understand the problem of the broken relationship with God because of sin, the helplessness to restore that relationship through anything we might do, and how Jesus was God's acceptable sacrifice for our sin? Are they ready to confess their sinful nature and ask God's forgiveness for sin? Do they believe in Jesus as the One sent from God who suffered and died for our sins, in our place, and arose again, so we can have salvation? Instruct these who make early decisions to be patient until their fellow listeners are able also to understand the Gospel as they do and are ready to follow Jesus.

Nearing Closure to the Evangelism Track

Be looking for signs of responsiveness during the Old Testament stories. Pay close attention to growing signs of responsiveness as the stories of Jesus move toward the Crucifixion and Resurrection stories. In reports of early use of Chronological Bible Teaching in the Philippines, listeners came under conviction of their sinfulness during the Old Testament stories. This was again illustrated in the "*Ee-taow!*" video account of the *Mouk* people in Papua New

Guinea when the listeners were heard to say, "We are like that!"[35]

Responsiveness may result from growing interest in the stories of Jesus. In places where the JESUS Film[36] was screened in India viewers were astounded that such bad things happened to a good man. This provided opportunity to explain why these things happened and who was to benefit. Where the Passion Story of Jesus was shared as a continuing story beginning with the Triumphal Entry to the Resurrection and Ascension, listeners came under a deep sense of remorse because of what happened. When they heard what the followers of Jesus did—how the followers like Thomas now believed and like Peter understood—they were ready to express their belief that the story was true and that God caused it to happen because of their sin. Like the Samaritan woman and her people, they too were ready to confess that Jesus is the Savior come into the world.

In the Bible Storying model sets that I have shared with others there is a deliberate increase in emphasis upon the coming events in the life of Jesus and what we should do in response. The Pre-Story Dialog diagnostic questions open up the issue of sin and who alone is able to forgive it.

Responsiveness may surface in the Post-Story Dialog time following the stories when the facts of the stories are reviewed and the implications of the stories are discussed. There is a fine line between pushing or urging listeners to do what you the storyer believe they should do and what the Spirit is leading the listeners to do. This requires patience for the response to come. This is a time of intense prayer by the storyer for the Holy Spirit to overcome any work of Satan and any hindrance that may be giving confusion or holding the listeners back from a growing awareness of their need to find salvation in Christ.

In the Evangelism Track story set different "drawing the net" stories have been used to bring listeners to a point of decision. For many it is the Ascension story when the angels tell that Jesus will return one day. Some Muslims have needed the Judgment stories to deal with certain worldview issues they have regarding the End Times and who will lead them to salvation. Some of the stories that have proven effective are the parable of the Prodigal Son (with its themes of repentance and acceptance), the story of the Rich Man and Lazarus (with its warning about failing to heed the words of the Prophets), the parable of the Great Banquet (when the guests declined the invitation), the Flood or Sodom and Gomorrah stories (with their judgment and obedience themes), and even the Calming of the Storm (with its themes of peace and faith).

People in the part of the world where I worked, and especially rural people, do not respond well to formula presentations of salvation or propositional types of presentations. They respond better to a story and identify with persons in the story who are like them in some way, who make a decision or profess their faith in Jesus—*i.e.*, Zacchaeus, the Woman Who Anointed the Feet of Jesus, the Samaritan woman, or the Man Born Blind in John 9. Even the story of the Prodigal Son can provoke response by presenting a drama with which listeners can readily identify because of the theme of filial piety. The parable of the Great Banquet in Luke 14 has been effective in setting up the invitation. Listeners are astounded that those invited should refuse the invitation to eat. After telling the story I comment that salvation is like that banquet—it is all prepared and the invitations have gone out. Whether to accept or reject the invitation is up to us. In the rural Asian world sharing a meal is the peak of hospitality and to reject such an invitation is a shameful thing to do. In Jacob Loewen's account of sharing stories with the Choco people, the people expressed their desire "to give God the hand and begin walking on God's road."[37] I often used the term "Become a follower of Jesus" among Muslim background listeners rather than "Become a Christian" because of strong negative connotation about what being a Christian meant.

Still other storyers choose to end the Bible stories, then use one of the propositional Scripture plans to sum up the issues of sin and helplessness and the promises of salvation for those who believe. Most storyers from the U.S.A. have at one time or another learned a propositional salvation scripture presentation. From a cultural standpoint, understand that many listeners who hear the stories do not logically reason as we do, and so may not respond as we think they ought. This is not to say don't use such a witness plan. If it logically works, use it. But be prepared to be more relational than logical if needed in your invitation to draw the net. Be prepared to illustrate the Scripture propositions with stories if needed.

A colleague storyer in Indonesia preferred to use a true Indonesian story to illustrate judgment and salvation. Some have used their own testimony of coming to faith in Jesus. Many have screened the JESUS Film which has the excellent recap at the end. How to draw the net is influenced by listeners' worldviews and to some extent by their culture.

When Response Is Slow In Coming

Not understanding the personal implications of the stories or realizing that all the stories are leading to the time of decision for Christ aren't the only reasons for delay. Actual persecution and fear of persecution are often lurking in the background of listeners. Those who live in oral communal societies do not live independent lives as we might imagine in our Western worldview. In oral societies it is not good to be out of line. Because of this, listeners may hold back until they see how other listeners respond. This is especially true where communal elders make the major decisions for the people. No one would make an independent decision for Christ, but they would readily join in the decision that their elders and peers make. For this reason every effort is made to share the Bible stories with a whole community rather than only to isolated individuals who express a curiosity or interest.

In LaNette Thompson's *Diaradugu Diary* she relates:

> There were five women in my group, the regulars. One woman, Koritimi, who is almost always there, is having to work. Safira is definitely there and places her stool right in front of me. Her married daughter and Fati are also there....They are very excited. I do not do the final storying lessons, but go directly into the lesson that Marvin has prepared on the plan of salvation. I talk about the necessity of believing that Jesus is the Son of God, that he came to earth, died, and was resurrected, of

knowing we are sinners, of asking forgiveness for our sins, of leaving the old things behind and being willing to follow Jesus. They listen intently and answer all the questions I ask. I say they must make the decision. I read in the Gospel of John where Jesus said that he might bring people out of darkness into the light. They shook their heads. They understood.

I looked at Safira. 'Do you believe all that I have said, do you want to follow Jesus?' 'Yes,' she shakes her head eagerly. 'I want to follow Jesus.' I turn to the next woman, Kadia, and repeat the same question. 'Yes,' she replies without hesitation. I ask Safira's daughter. 'Yes,' she replies. I turn to Fati with the same question. She turns her head away. Kadia talks to her. I don't understand all she says, but she is talking about Jesus. Fati still shakes her head. Safira touches my arm and says, 'Continue.' I turn to the next woman, Diarata, and ask her. 'Yes,' she replies. I explained that I wanted to make sure they had made the decision themselves and to show that, if they really wanted to follow Jesus, then they must stand up. One by one, with Safira first, they stood up — four women. Fati did not stand. Then I led them in the sinner's prayer. They repeated the prayer after me. Following the prayer we shook hands and I talked about how to grow as a Christian.

Koritimi comes running up. It is obvious she has rushed through her work in order to come meet me. I can tell by her manner she is ready to make a decision. She sits beside me. And once more I go through the plan of salvation and ask if she wants to make a commitment. She says, 'Yes.' We pray, she repeats what I say. Her joy is obvious. Another woman comes up, I do not know her. I asked if she had seen the (*JESUS*) film. She says yes and it really pleased her. I asked if

> she wanted to follow Jesus, but she looked away. It is the five women who have been in the storying sessions who have made decisions."[38]

LaNette's husband Marvin had disappointment with the lack of response among his men. Later as Marvin and LaNette returned to the village to tell the people good-bye, LaNette writes:

> "As we get in the truck, Marvin says, 'I don't even know why I'm going. It is obvious the men aren't ready to make a commitment yet. I don't know what else to do. I can't go forward, and I can't keep reviewing the same stories. It's up to them, now.' About two kilometers from the village we see a man standing by the side of the road. It is Mahama, the *delegué*. He is standing ramrod stiff, his short-handled hoe hanging from his shoulder. We stop the truck and Marvin gets out to greet him. As Marvin approaches Mahama, he holds out his hand to greet Mahama. But Mahama does not take Marvin's hand. Instead, he throws his hoe to the ground and flings both arms around Marvin and hugs him. We are astonished as this is not done in African culture. Mahama is trembling.
>
> "I've been waiting for you here because I knew you would come today and I wanted to speak to you privately,' he began. 'I had to tell you. I've been going over all of those stories you've been telling us. I've read some of them myself. I had to tell you, I have seen the truth. The truth is Jesus!' Tears filled his eyes. 'I cannot tell my people now. If I do, they will chase me from the village. But I think by harvest time they will have seen the change in me, and I can tell them then. But I knew I had to tell you, and to say thank you.'"[39]

These accounts are not uncommon reactions. Not all the women responded to the invitation. There is more to that story in that the women later became fearful about telling their husbands what they had done. Among the men there was no immediate response to Marvin's invitation. Mahama, the *delegué* was the spokesman for the men. Marvin was elated to learn of Mahama's decision but it was a private decision to be revealed to the others when the right time came.

For many of the listeners the promise of daily suffering ending at some future time when they go to heaven is beyond their comprehension. They live in the here and now. Tomorrow is a long way off. They respond better to emphasis of forgiveness for sin right now with the prospect of peace and blessing now coming from a right relationship with God through Jesus Christ. Among rural people in India the invitation was for God's Peace to quiet the suffering heart rather than going to heaven when they die. Many had only a vague idea of sin but actually struggled under a burden of unforgiveness that needed to be lifted. Among many Muslim women, I found that going to heaven was not attractive, as that was a place for men to enjoy. But if salvation were presented as a possible relationship and acceptance by God that was made possible through Jesus, it was desirable. God could redeem their lives.

You the storyer will need to pray, asking for wisdom how best to present closure to the evangelism story. What kind of an invitation will speak to the listeners and be one to which they can culturally respond? In some situations you may not be able to ask for a visible response to the presentation of the gospel. If so, you may want to ask the listeners to make the decision in their hearts and ask God to help them be bold to share it at the right time. In the story models for Muslim women, I suggested several ways in which listeners might share their decisions privately with the storyer, realizing that at some point the decision must be shared with husbands, other wives, other relatives, and the community as the Holy Spirit gives boldness. If listeners are reluctant to signal their faith in Jesus publicly, they may be permitted to whisper their decision to the storyer. Where fear is deeply rooted, the storyer has suggested encouraging each listener in their hearts to make a silent profession of their faith in Christ, and promise to make that decision public when the Holy Spirit gives boldness and courage. Among many people groups one is not considered to have converted until baptism. So people can profess their faith and as long as they are not baptized there is little concern.

Group Decisions

Group decisions happen. When listeners respond as a group, especially after one of their elders has done so, it is good to provide several stories in which characters express their individual faith. Stories like the Samaritan Woman, Martha's confession at the Raising of Lazarus, and from Acts the response of the people from Peter's Sermon, or the Philippian Jailer when he asked, "What must I do to be saved?" model ways in which listeners can respond. This is to remind the listeners that while their group have made this joint decision, that each listener has an individual responsibility to express his/her own faith in Jesus.

Post Closure Dialog and Late Responders

There are often late responders who, for whatever reason, were prevented from making a decision for Christ at the time of closure invitation. So be prepared to leave the door open for these people when they are finally able to resolve in their hearts what is right to do. Also be prepared to go back and review selected story lessons as a way of strengthening these brothers and sisters who are struggling with the problem of sin, and confused by the teaching from the prevailing religion about who Jesus is.

Immediate and Continuing Affirmation Needed

Satan will be hard at work trying to confuse listeners and hinder their being able to see the light of the Gospel. For those who do make a decision for Christ, they will need immediate affirmation that they have made the right decision. There are several ways to do this. One is to go back over selected stories that deal with sin and forgiveness, and the work of Jesus to show they have made the right decision. Another is to take a different tack of involving new believers in immediate witness and intercessory prayer for others needing to believe in Jesus. Memory verses and commencing discipling lessons help to stabilize the new believers. They will have questions about this new life in Christ and need additional Scripture verses which give assurance and guidance.

Baptism of New Believers

The best way to approach the matter of baptism is through the baptism stories in Acts so that at some point someone should ask, "Why haven't we been baptized? We believe like these people!" It is also helpful to explain about the meaning of the symbolism of baptism as a picture of the washing away of sins, death, and burial of the old person, and rising in newness of life in Christ, obedience to Christ's command, and as a testimony of one's faith in Christ and identification with him publicly. Rather than just teaching on these themes it is helpful to illustrate with stories. It often is best to wait until several can be baptized at the same time for mutual strengthening. In some of the places where I told the stories, I was asked not to be present during baptism to prevent the accusation that a foreigner was converting the people.

Beginning Worship and Developing a Community of Faith

For the Gospel to take root a church must be planted and it must grow and be a reproducing church, contributing to the spread of the kingdom among a people. The Acts stories give a model of what believers did in that day after Jesus returned to heaven. A tension will develop between the former ways of prayer, ritual, worship, and meeting the new expectation in Christ.

It is important for listeners to become believers before leading them to become a church. If there is not a significant or majority response to drawing the net, it may be helpful to go back through the major Evangelism Track stories. This review is good for the late responders and for those joining the group late. This can contribute to a tension to plant the church and quickly leave. But taking this time to review may significantly reduce future syncretism when partially-evangelized listeners are swept into a newly planted church and mixed with saved believers who are already growing in their faith.

For more thoughts on this process of planting a New Testament church and encouraging the beginning of a Church Planting Movement, and a look at some of the issues related to why this may be slow in happening, see the book by Terry and Sanchez, *Chronological Bible Storying and Church Planting Movements*, Church Starting Network. (www.churchstarting.net)

Chapter 17

Teaching Pictures and Other Media

When Chronological Bible Teaching and Storying were being shared between mission agencies in the Philippines, the groups agreed to produce jointly a set of Bible pictures to accompany the Bible teaching for tribal peoples. International Mission Board and New Tribes Mission collaborated to develop a set of 103 high-detail color pictures and two maps of the Bible world. This set of 13 by 17 inch "Telling the Story..."[40] color pictures was immediately popular when used in the Philippines with tribal viewers of low visual literacy. To accommodate their low visual literacy, the number of people in each picture was reduced to a minimum and very little perspective was used to depict depth or distance from the viewer. Those consulting on the project chose at what point to depict the story scene and whether one or several pictures were required for each story.

Few problems arose in using the pictures among those for whom the set was developed. But later, when sets of the pictures were shipped to neighboring countries where different cultures and worldviews existed, some of the pictures proved to be too bold, especially the Adam and Eve pictures, due to a realistic depiction of the unclothed Eve. In other pictures where Jesus was alone with the Samaritan woman, this was socially offensive to some. Dress lengths and bare legs were a problem for some Muslim viewers. More conservative Muslims did not at first like depiction of the prophets' faces or the crucifixion.

The set was expensive at US $25. It was a helpful set for most missionaries to use but when many local storyers were being trained, the cost became prohibitive. In addition, the pictures quickly became worn in constant use and some were lost, so frequent replacement was necessary.

When I began to teach the Bible stories in other South Asian countries, I used those "Telling the Story...." pictures by displaying them clipped to a line strung across the teaching area. As each new story was told in training sessions I added another picture or two. When we stopped for tea or meals and then resumed, I used the string of pictures quickly to review the previous stories before adding a new story picture.

On the humorous side I used plastic clothes pins to attach the pictures to the line. Apparently I introduced a new concept in clothes drying to the area. Where we were teaching for several days and the men slept in the building at night, I would find their laundry attached to the line to dry overnight! In the Philippines where at that time the Betamax video players were common, the picture strings were often referred to as a "*betaimax*" playing upon the local word for "string."

In those first days of Bible Storying the local missions decided to give each trainee a set of the "Telling the Story..." pictures. Later I discovered that some of the trainees took the pictures home as souvenirs of their training but never used them. Others found that the pictures were nice to decorate their homes. Because the set of 105 pieces of coated paper was very heavy and the cardboard storage sleeve was not sturdy, the pictures soon became damaged or individual pictures lost.

My Filipino mentor who taught Bible Storying to tribal youths in the Philippines had opted to make black and white line drawing traces of the "Telling the Story..." pictures and provided a crude light box so the tribal trainees could trace their own sets of pictures and hand color them. Later an artist made better quality black and white line drawings from the color pictures and these were published in letter size at a very low cost. The black and white line drawings were less offensive to some conservative Muslims than the high detail color pictures and found early acceptance in West Africa. The pictures are available in both formats today from New Tribes Bookstore in Sanford, Florida.[41]

Several advantages accompany the use of teaching pictures:

- *Pictures provide a visualization of the story at some key point(s) in the storyline. The storyer, however, must decide if the point(s) the story scenes depict are the best illustration for the story.*

- *Pictures provide a visualization of unfamiliar objects such as the ark in Noah's day, the Ark of the Covenant, the Cross, and altars with sacrifices.*
- *Pictures provide a focal point of interest for the listeners so that hopefully all are seeing the scenes at the same time and so are not sitting there struggling mentally to construct an unfamiliar visual scene.*
- *Pictures can help to connect stories if the same recognizable characters appear in them. In the "Telling the Story..." set Abraham has the same color clothing in the Old Testament stories and again in the story of The Rich Man and Lazarus where he appears. A series of pictures provides continuity of stories and illustrates changes in characters.*
- *Possessing pictures has given boldness to some who are timid to tell the stories. Sets of simple pictures have been helpful for non-literate "Biblewomen" to cue them as what story to tell and to give the listeners a visual to study.*
- *Pictures have value in "qualifying" those too young to teach elders because they have something the elders do not possess.*
- *Pictures, if they are culturally contextualized, can help to reduce the "foreignness" of a story as the scenes and people with their clothing look like the listeners.*
- *Pictures are wonderful for reviewing previous stories. Once a story is told and a picture associated with the story, then displaying the picture triggers recall of the associated story.*

Limitations and disadvantages in the use of teaching pictures when telling Bible stories also arise.

- *Pictures can and do introduce unwanted cultural elements and may actually disturb telling the story. In the "Telling the Story..." set the Samaritan Woman and Jesus are alone at the well in the original picture. This was disturbing to some as Jesus and the woman were not married and no one else was present. Later the disciple Andrew was added in the background. The woman's dress needed to be lengthened to a more appropriate length to cover her ankles.*

- *Some cultures like the Hindu peoples of Bangladesh prefer near photographic quality picture sets like "Telling the Story..." Less costly sets were available in the country but were said to be "cartoonish" and so rejected by Bengali viewers.*
- *Some of Muslim religious worldview are offended by immodest dress of the women, depicting prophet's faces, and especially depicting Jesus. This is less of a problem today after many years of screening the JESUS Film in these areas. Where teaching pictures offend viewers I suggest not using them.*
- *Initial cost of picture sets and maintenance of the sets by users can be a burden. One of the objectives of Bible Storying was to provide a field reproducible witness and discipling methodology. Using pictures places a budget limitation on how many storyers can be trained and deployed with picture sets.*
- *One of the real limitations is that when the story set is picture-driven then only the stories that have accompanying pictures can be told. If no pictures are used, then the storyer has greater freedom of choice in the stories used.*
- *Some among non-literate storyers being trained had difficulty in telling the story and referring to the picture in an appropriate manner. Most wanted to stand and describe the picture which distracted them from telling the story.*
- *Some picture sets had the story plot depicted either in an inaccurate manner or at the wrong point in the storyline. One set of pictures I have used depicts Noah and his sons building the ark framework but there was no picture of the flood or post-flood sacrifice. In another set the ark is floating on a mirror smooth pool of blue water; there was no turbulence, no people or animals struggling in the water to save their lives, so the judgment theme was lost. The*

Jonah story had only Jonah and the fish but not Jonah running away or the people of Nineveh repenting.

- *Paper pictures are fragile and easily torn. New Tribes solved this by laminating the pictures which does vastly increase their life but adds to the weight and cost, and makes it difficult to carry the rigid pictures rolled in a map case or PVC tube like a quiver.*
- *A last point that is very important is that of modeling for storyers. I had used teaching pictures in my early training of storyers only to learn later that most had not told the stories because "they had no pictures!" As a compromise in providing pictures for everyone I assigned several storyers to the same set of pictures since not all the pictures were needed by each storyer at the same time. This also helped to police the picture set as each user was concerned that no pictures be lost. I still had to occasionally replace a picture by having color photocopies made from my master set.*

I vividly remember an elderly man in Africa in one of our sessions. I had shared about using pictures. Later he said to me: "If you tell a story well you don't need a picture!"

When a twenty picture set of re-colorized black-and-white line drawings was done for use among the *Kui*, the pictures were arranged four to a letter size page, printed on card stock, laminated, and loosely bound in the correct order. The four pictures on each page were based on pictures developed by a Filipino storyer to accompany his teaching materials.[42] Back in the Philippines rural missionaries had the same pictures reproduced by a soft drink company on a large, roadside banner which could be displayed over the road to advertise a Bible Storying revival. Each night the banner would be taken down and folded to display the four-picture pane that accompanied the stories to be told that night.

The "*Telling the Story...*" picture set had a cutaway view of inside the Tabernacle Tent. It was difficult for viewers to understand that the tent really had a side but that it was removed in the picture to reveal the inside. Later I found a cardboard model of the Tabernacle and related objects. The

Tabernacle was assembled so that the top could be removed to see what was inside. I had taught about the Holy Place and the Holy of Holies where only the high priest could enter once each year to make sacrifice for the sins of the people. When some of the listeners came to inspect the model I removed the top of the tent so they could see inside. One of the men cautioned me that I should not do that as only the high priest was allowed to look inside!

Besides models like the Tabernacle, one can use teaching objects. In the "*Ee-taow*!" video Mark Zook told the story of Abraham and Isaac while holding a toy sheep and a knife in his hands. Models of the Ten Commandment stone tablets or Noah's ark and other objects have been used to illustrate stories.

Some have used flannelgraph sets like the Betty Lukens *Through the Bible in Felt*[43] that comes with instructions for telling 150 stories but with a little imagination can be used for most stories in the Bible. Cost is a factor though the activity of building the picture as the story is told provides a powerful dynamic illustration for viewers.

Bible timeline charts have been used some with students and literate professionals. I do not recommend them for use with typical non-literate rural listeners who not only can't read the words on the chart but usually have difficulty making sense of the timeline.

At this point let me go back to the issue of cultural or social appropriateness of media, especially pictures. One of the questions commonly raised is that of whether contextualization is helpful or hurtful. One set of pictures I purchased while in Africa is the *Life of Jesus Mafa* set of the story of Jesus.[44] Jesus and all the people are depicted as Africans, in African clothing, and taking place in African scenes common to Cameroon. Those who object say that Jesus was not African and this is inaccurate. Those who developed the pictures thought it important that the Africans see Jesus as "like them" and not as a "white European."

I have another set purchased in India of both the Old and New Testament stories where Jesus and all the people are depicted as Indian. Indian conventions are used for depicting angels, Jesus as a guru is in a saffron robe, and other typical scenes familiar to Indian audiences. In addition, cost was very nominal and the set was available in India so did not need importing. Another set from Cambodia depicts Jesus and the people as distinctly Cambodian. A black-and-white line drawing set from a Chinese book depicted Jesus and the people dressed in 19th Century Chinese clothing and scenes.

A more recent set from North India was highly contextualized, depicting the Bible scenes more like those found in North Indian temples. In Nepal the story of Jesus was depicted in the *Wheel of Life* much like the Buddhist Wheel of Life *thangka* paintings. The point is this: Contextualization can reduce the foreignness of the story as it is depicted. The people in the pictures look like those viewing the pictures. Stories with contextualized pictures are easier to be viewed as relevant for listeners.

One last thought regarding using any visual media like teaching pictures, flannelgraph sets, or even hand-held objects should be sounded. Be certain to test their appropriateness. If not appropriate, or if there is confusion from the visual or rejection of the visual, don't use it.

The *JESUS Film* as well as several other videos of the Bible story of Jesus' life all have value for visualization of the stories. For some, the *JESUS Film* provided the visualized recap of the story of Jesus used in "Drawing the Net." For others the *JESUS Film* benefited by telling the Old Testament stories before the film that pointed toward the story of Jesus.

Devices like DVD players are now beginning to replace videotape machines in many places. Some have even used video projectors where stable electric power makes this possible. Remember modeling and realize that a tension always exists between modeling reproducibility and whatever expediency value the visual adds to the storytelling event.

Audiocassettes and more recently audio CDs are being used. In Thailand listeners liked the recorded story as the "machine always told the story the same way every time!" Missionaries have benefited from having a competent local storyteller record the Bible story for playing in the storying session. A copy of the audiocassette can be left with the listeners after the storying session.

Now digital players like the *Ambassador* by MegaVoice[45] or the *Proclaimer* by Faith Comes By Hearing[46] make possible playback of story sets without the problem of damaged audiocassettes or their being over-recorded. In addition, players like the Ambassador can be recharged by built-in solar panel. Now a field unit is available for reloading the digital file or updating it.

Digital and audiocassette players and CDs can be sent in where missionaries cannot go. In addition, the players can be left with a people so they can continue to listen to learn the stories and to refresh the stories to lessen story drifting. Use of these digital players could be an important aspect of a Bible storying strategy for an unreached people.

Story sets like the Evangelism Track and Discipling Track are being put on audiocassette or CD for distribution. Once an adequate recording is made, it can then be reproduced and distributed. The most comprehensive audio model now on CD is the *Following Jesus*[47] discipleship stories which contain an Evangelism Track and a complete spectrum of discipleship stories in seven modules. The initial set was done in English and is being translated into several major languages.

Bible Storying over radio is another possibility to support a Bible Storying strategy. There are other considerations when preparing and broadcasting Bible stories to overcome the lack of face-to-face presence. A future booklet will address some of these issues and give counsel on preparation and recording of Bible stories for broadcast.

Visual and audio media are wonderful tools, adjuncts to the Bible storytelling process. Just remember that stories can be told by a person without any of these devices or materials. If modeling reproducibility is the primary objective, then consider what is least costly, most easily available locally, and most appropriate contextually while retaining accuracy of the story. Ask yourself, What do you gain and what do you lose by using the media?

Chapter 18
Bible Storying Toolbox

Bible Storying is more than a single format and delivery method for teaching the Bible. Bible Storying began as a lengthy strategy for telling Bible stories chronologically as a method for evangelism, discipling, church planting, and leadership development, but it is more. These early lessons sets typically consisted of thirty-five or more evangelism stories which were usually taught one or more a week over the engagement time frame, and then continued additional Bible story lessons to plant the church, begin discipling new believers, train emerging leaders and new Bible storyers. A full set of stories might require two years to cover by teaching one lesson a week. It was a long commitment for many missionaries to make due to their family needs, various mission activities, stateside assignments, local holidays, interruptions for food distribution during famines, and the weather—particularly rainy seasons which made roads difficult to travel and hindered public meetings. Where interruptions did occur during longer Chronological Bible Storying strategies missionaries found that extensive review or even the need to start over was required. It was also a long commitment for many oral listeners to make as well due to various needs in their lives, their observance and participation in holiday festivities, interruptions and mourning for deaths, and especially the agricultural season for farmers and following grazing needs for those who were shepherds. But the slow pace favored oral learners because of its much repetition and time for reflection about each story.

Another matter was the lack of urgency that the longer storying strategies permitted. This was noted by some missionaries in West Africa who felt there was a disconnect between the urgency of the salvation message and the slow delivery over a long period of time. This storyer has also noted a greater tendency for listeners to sense urgency with fewer stories. Newer Bible Storying strategies then tend to favor the shorter story sets delivered in a more urgent manner to encourage greater listener sense of urgency.

New Needs Arose

Storyers soon discovered that many new needs and opportunities arose to present Bible stories in much more limited time frames and with more directed focus to meet particular ministry needs. Among those emerging needs and newly discovered opportunities were:

There is a general need for shorter or more compact Bible story sets rather than the lengthy traditional story sets initially used in early Chronological Bible Storying strategies

- The need for shorter or more compact story sets to be used during radio listener rallies that could be completed in hours, not weeks or months.
- Telling the Old Testament stories leading up to Christ for introducing the JESUS Film to those who needed the biblical OT perspective in order to understand the story of Jesus.
- Opportunities to enter homes to pray for sick persons and for other family needs continued to arise. These opportunities then led to additional times with families (and neighbors) when they insisted on providing refreshments or a meal for the storying evangelists. This they did as a thank you for the prayer on behalf of the family. These opportunity windows often lasted as long as two-to-three hours for sharing evangelism stories of Jesus.
- Still more opportunities opened up as brief bedside presentations in hospital wards for patient visitation. The first request for such a hospital set of stories came from an International Mission Board missionary serving at the Baptist hospital in Sumatra, Indonesia.
- Training new Bible storyers pointed to a need to give the trainees a fast-track overview of the larger Bible Redemption Story. This gave a biblical perspective before going back to explore each individual story, what was learned from the story, how to tell each story, and teach from it.
- The Fast-track presentation initially grew out of several opportunities such as *JESUS Film* and radio-

listener rally presentations, redeeming the time with families while waiting for them to serve a hospitality meal, and Bible panorama overviews during storyer training.

- Ministry projects like medical, eyeglass and dental clinics provided additional opportunity for shorter presentations which might or might not be chronological in organization. Clinic waiting-room presentations of only the Bible stories could be recorded and played over and over.
- Development projects like water projects provided opportunity to story thematically to those who came to watch or work in the project.
- Ministry needs existed to provide Bible Storying that served to comfort and assure populations of God's love and providence after disasters like earthquakes, storms, floods or tsunami, while urging upon them the need to know Jesus as their Savior. *Hope Stories from the Bible*[48] is one such example.

Many of these above-mentioned needs primarily called for thematically arranged Bible stories which might or might not follow a chronological timeline. Some situations emerged where a story set was taken from a single Gospel or there was need to begin with the story of Jesus (for various reasons) before going back to pick up the foundational stories in the Old Testament.

A recent phenomenon has been a return to shorter generic chronological-story tracks utilizing basic Bible stories that are not necessarily worldview sensitive. The generic tracks have been typically around twenty to twenty-four stories in length (or less). Each track might be delivered in story clusters of several stories at one session or one story at a time with brief post-story discussion.

For want of a better term this approach has been called *short-tracking* as it is still generally chronological in organization, but fitting into a more compact time frame. Short-term missionaries whose witness opportunities and time frame in a country have been limited are using extremely short micro-tracks of ten or fewer stories. One representative micro-track of stories was done for Hindu women[49] at the request of a short-term missionary.

A new potential use of a short-term story set has been in personal ministry like *Lifestory Conversations*[50] in which appropriate Bible stories have been used in ministry exchange during a conversational or casual sharing of personal stories. This has often reflected a personal need or hurt. The exchange has been "your story," "my story," and "God's story." This requires having some of God's stories ready to tell. A soon to be published book will develop this concept with suggestions and examples for the use of personal and Bible stories in conversational encounters.

Bible stories can be used in other unique ways. One is a Luke Model in which a condensed story of Jesus is shared in a letter to someone that you have had contact with during travel or a mission trip. While people are getting away from writing letters in the U.S., there is still great value in letters as messages among those who live in other places. A variation of this would be to spread the stories out over a series of letters. I like to use the personal biblical style greeting (like Paul used in his Epistles) and then after some relational sharing continue with the stories. Also Bible stories can be written into or attached inside greeting cards sent for birthdays, Christmas or Easter. These have a long shelf life as I have found my greeting cards on display in homes I visited months later. Cards are valued.

Fig 4. Strategic Bible Storying Tools

Development of the Bible Storying Tool Box Concept

The idea of a Storying Tool Box emerged in which there were both ***strategic*** and ***tactical*** storying tools serving different but related functions.

Strategic refers to a larger (longer) more inclusive plan or multiple interrelated plans that might reach several objectives in succession. A story strategy is conducted over a longer period of time and consists of several successive story tracks, each with their specific objectives. The tracks are driven by an overarching objective of initiating a potential church-planting movement among a people group. This used Bible Storying to teach about one's accountability to God, the effect of sin and its penalty, and the salvation God has prepared through faith in Jesus as Savior.

The initial objective is to engage a people and evangelize them with culturally relational and worldview-sensitive Bible story lessons. Upon reaching the Cross and having professions of faith, the next objective is to move on to Acts story lessons to plant a church. Discipling story lessons continue to mature and stabilize believers in their faith. Additional story lessons provide training for emerging church leaders and training of new storyers to continue the evangelism process among their people. The strategy is to initiate a potential church-planting movement. Multiple tracks, each using Bible Storying, move the strategy along toward the CPM goal.

In contrast, ***tactical*** refers to a more limited engagement that is often one-on-one, or at least much smaller scale, brief, and has a limited objective that relates to the immediate encounter or listener need. Tactical encounters quite often are component parts of larger strategic plans or can serve to initiate them by locating and cultivating responsiveness among a previously unreached people. Once responsiveness is established then the strategic plan takes over and the tactical moves to find new listeners.

Tactical storying could take any of several forms which might or might not be chronological in nature. Among the short forms of chronological presentation, one-on-one Bible Storying using pocket picture sets is a tactical approach. Taking advantage of a ministry opportunity in a home to share one or more appropriate Bible stories is another helpful tactic. There are many more as you will soon see.

Looking at the many possibilities of Bible Storying then gives a clear picture of both strategic and tactical uses of storying that are like tools best at performing certain tasks at certain times and with certain listeners. Your task as a Bible storyer is to select the best Storying Tool needed for the moment or objective. Knowing the advantages of each tool and being prepared to make use of any one as needed will keep storying tools sharp and ready to use.

Chronological Bible Storying

Chronological Bible Storying (CBS) is clearly a strategy in that it is a larger multi-track approach that includes reaching a number of objectives through objective-focused, sequential story-teaching tracks which include evangelism, planting a church, discipling, and initial emerging leader training. It could include the shadowing strategy of giving an Oral Bible which nicely parallels the main evangelism and discipling strategy. Chronological Bible Storying works well if world-view-sensitive but is always primarily driven by Bible truth leading to the teaching objective.

Chronological Bible Storying sessions can grow out of initial tactical-storying encounters that probe for responsiveness among a people. The CBS strategy is cyclic and self-perpetuating in that each Bible Storying cycle has the potential of generating new Bible-Storying cycles by attracting new listeners in the same location, invitations to story in new locations, and by generating new Bible storyers. Through modeling in teaching and deliberate leader training it achieves competency in story knowledge and story lesson teaching. So in that realm it is supportive of moving toward a church planting movement.

Chronological Bible Storing uses verbatim and crafted Bible stories in the mother tongue as the primary means of teaching. This method also employs appropriate reproducible teaching exercises. The approach provides the possibility for non-literate and oral learner peoples to be able to reproduce the Bible teaching with its story core through reasonable accuracy and an Oral Bible as well.

Length of the initial strategy cycle is dependent upon the window of teaching opportunity for both listeners and storyer. Also entering into the strategy is the combination of criteria derived from the Bible Truths that needed emphasis and any priority worldview issues which are barriers to the Gospel and Church. Long strategies need more review along the way to prevent story fading before the closure stories.

Complaints that CBS took "too long" and was "overkill" arose occasionally. This criticism surfaced when someone other than the storyer thought that a much shorter teaching track could accomplish the same results. While true for some situations where listeners proved more knowledgeable or responsive than anticipated, there were many people groups among the several major religions whose significant spiritual worldview issues required the longer tracks.

Several pressures drove the "short-tracking" approach. Among these pressures were strategic and administrative needs to get to Church and CPM sooner without the potentially long delay from a lengthy CBS track. There was a need to shorten the relationship time required by missionaries due to stateside assignments, family needs, and other field responsibilities requiring absence from the storying scene that could result in unfinished storying tracks. Limited access to listeners due to difficult geographical location, seasonal weather, government or hostile religious leader interference provide reasons for short-tracking during the window of opportunity. Some storyers are finding that their national trainees are having difficulty in coping with the longer and more complex evangelism tracks which require a long commitment of many sessions to finish the track. Also the longer tracks appeared to blunt a sense of urgency to tell the stories to others.

Chronological Bible Storying Short-Tracking

Chronological Bible Storying—*Short-Tracking* is a variant of CBS that actually has roots in earlier versions of short generic sets of Bible stories. One set used in India in the Calcutta area some years ago was *Twenty-Four Bible Stories for Village Workers.*[51] In the Philippines, *The Witnessing Kit,*[52] became popular as a short model of twenty-story lessons accompanied by teaching pictures. A missionary working among a tribal group in the southern Philippines used nine-story lessons which included several story clusters for a total of twenty-nine stories but all taught within the time frame of nine sessions.[53]

A historical model used in Panama among the Chocos in the 1950s and recounted in "*Bible Stories: Message and Matrix*"[54] used twenty-four stories selected according to criteria related to biblical truth and worldview. A more recent model of the very short variety is Christy Brawner's[55] "*Good News of Jesus*" (seven stories from Matthew's Gospel) and its discipling companion "*Beginning a New Life in Christ*" (eight stories from Matthew's Gospel). A popular model is the West African *Storying Scarf*[56] which features twenty-one stories selected primarily for Muslim listeners.

The *short-track* approach relied on a generic worldview and a story mix that gave a balance of focus on Old Testament stories and stories of Jesus according to listeners' preexisting knowledge about Jesus and understanding of one's accountability to God for sin. Generally, as the tracks got shorter, the balance shifted toward a greater ratio of stories about Jesus. *Short-tracks* can be expanded by utilizing story clusters at each session to strengthen emphasis on needed biblical truths or worldview issues. These truths or worldview issues need addressing while not increasing the total number of teaching sessions.

One variant of the *short-track* proposed using a team of three storyers to teach seven stories at a time in three consecutive storying sessions for a total of twenty-one stories. Team members shared several stories each session. This was apparently more manageable, the team provided accountability to finish the track, and led in dialog to draw the net after all the stories are told.

Reliance on *short-track* storying models in some circumstances could result in unresolved worldview issues leading to syncretism or might fail to provide the needed depth of teaching to reach the evangelism objective.

Chronological Bible Storytelling

Chronological Bible Storytelling (CBSt) is a hybrid that grew out of the early shift of primary teaching *from the stories* to a primary focus on *telling the stories* as part of the teaching. Early models from the Philippines made use primarily of deeply paraphrased stories that were reworded (crafted) to emphasize truths being taught in a particular lesson. Paraphrasing might include the use of additional descriptive wording to create a setting, to more fully describe characters, and/or to add further emphasis to the actions or words in the narrative. The two most popular models in English are both backtranslations out of story lessons sets originally in Philippine languages. Any retranslation of either story set from English into another language involves distancing the story wording yet another generation away from the actual Bible wording.

Another *CBSt* format included embedded teaching within the paraphrased story in the form of comments, explanations, and rhetorical questions to give emphasis to the teaching points. This alternative proved popular in some areas where an Oral Bible is not an objective or listeners might be semiliterate and possess written Scriptures.

A third CBSt variation uses verbatim Scripture passage quotes as story but interrupts the narrative to insert teaching related to each portion of the passage. *The teaching from the story takes precedence over an intact telling of the story.* This latter form was generally very disturbing for those who are true oral learners. They prefer a complete uninterrupted telling of a story and who may confuse the inserted teaching as being part of the Bible story or consider the story fragments as separate stories.

The *CBSt* tracks, as in Chronological Bible Storying, serve to reach the same objectives of evangelism, discipling, and church planting. Among some CBSt users in Southeast Asia storying tracks are called "phases."

The CBSt model has value when used with literates familiar with the stories and who are not disturbed by the interrupted narratives and paraphrasing from the Scripture text. Where the storyer desires to provide an Oral Bible for non-literates, the paraphrased story is not as accurate as it had been manipulated to support the teaching. The interrupted story would be most objectionable with true oral learners.

In general Chronological Bible Storytelling is seldom the best approach with oral peoples. Some forms of it might not result in reproducible stories. There is always the danger that the expanded story, distorted by embedding teaching in the story, might become part of the Bible story for listeners and in doing so mislead listeners or give rise to a greater chance of story fragments.

Chronological Bible Teaching

Chronological Bible Teaching (CBT) is possible where the stories are well known by listeners and can be recalled by simply referring to them in the teaching or where the listeners are already literate or becoming literate. In its purest form the Bible stories might not be told as stories or, if told, there is little or no effort to teach the stories as stories for oral peoples. The focus is *primarily on the expositional teaching drawn from the stories.*

CBT can work well when used in a strategy with literate listeners who prefer more traditional expositional teaching and who can read the stories for themselves or participate in reading as a group. It is not uncommon for some of the major stories to be told and other passages simply explored but not narrated as story. Objectives remain the same as for Chronological Bible Storying. *The teaching drawn from the story takes precedence over telling the story.* Previous knowledge of the stories by literates is assumed from previous teaching or the stories can be accessed in their reading and are available in the mother tongue.

Generally Chronological Bible Teaching (*CBT*) is used because of the expositional teaching is reproducible best by literates. These readers can read from their notes or teaching materials supplied by the Bible storyer.

Where Bible translation and literacy are also part of the local strategy CBT has been used when the translated scriptures and lessons are read and taught by national workers.

Tactical Bible Storying Tools

Fast-Tracking as a method is telling a series of Bible stories one after another without stopping for discussion or review. The object is to cover the larger story for an overview or panorama to help listeners and trainees understand how the component stories fit together or to capture the maximum spiritual-emotional response from the progressing story.

- *Probing for evangelistic responsiveness with storying events in public places or in connection with other public events, market areas, under roadside tents, etc. This might be an established storying point in a public area or could be an impromptu storying between members of a storying team where one team member stories to others in the group within earshot of listeners who will be attracted to the stories.*
- *Testing worldview assumptions is used to select and craft most effective stories to be used in typical CBS strategies.*
- *Providing compact but intensive Bible teaching as a program event at broadcast media follow-up rallies for both evangelism and discipleship. This could be a full fast-track of stories or a condensed fast-track according to the time available and objective.*
- *Providing panoramic overviews of the Redemption Story for those being trained to tell Bible stories. The object is to give the overview and show the holistic picture of the larger linked Bible story before going story-by-story with appropriate teaching and practice to tell the individual stories.*
- *Providing Old Testament introduction before screening of JESUS Film. (Could also include pre-storying of Luke Jesus stories as a preview of the JESUS Film.) Storying might be done in one abbreviated session before the film or in several sessions preceding screening the film. The object is to prepare listeners to understand the story of Jesus by providing a background of events and prophecies leading up to the coming of Jesus.*
- *Providing compact evangelistic witness to families and neighbors when a storyer is invited to share a meal. This often follows prayer requested for a family need and reflects the family's gratitude for the ministry. Preparing a meal or refreshment can take a*

lengthy period of waiting while being prepared. Curious neighbors gather to see the visitor. Fast-track Bible Storying then is an excellent way to redeem the time and open the way for further witness.

- *Providing short, simple presentations bedside in hospital ministry. A set of pocket-sized Bible pictures makes a good portable visual to accompany stories. Story presentation is tailored to last a maximum of ten-fifteen minutes or so, usually covering in summary form about twelve-to-fifteen stories with pictures. Family members and other patients could be invited to listen. At the end of the presentation the patient is told that when he/she is well again and released from the hospital and has returned home they could invite someone to come and tell these and more stories for their family and neighbors.*
- *Providing soft witness to those of mixed spiritual background in hospital chapel services where patients and visitors attend. Visual presentations like large teaching pictures, preaching charts, and flannelgraph displays effectively illustrate the stories being told.*
- *Providing one-on-one evangelism storying using pocket picture books when traveling. This method at one time was included as part of people-powered media, that is, use of media in which a person instead of some piece of equipment is the message delivery system. Small photo-sized Bible teaching pictures can be put into a pocket photo album along with other suitable photos used to initiate an encounter which leads to evangelistic presentation. The pictures are used to illustrate the stories. Storying themes are generally "family oriented—my family, family of man, family of God, and how to be a part of God's family through faith in Jesus."*
- *Providing initial evangelistic encounter with the Family of Peace when using the Man of Peace strategy. While visiting in a "man of peace" home, if the storyer is asked what he/she does, the opportunity arises to say, "I'm a storyteller. Would you like to hear some of my stories?" If the family*

response is positive, an opportunity to tell Bible stories results. An invitation could be given for neighbors to join in hearing the stories. After an initial presentation to the family of peace, opportunities could open for other presentations among friends and additional neighbors.

- *Public story lectures of a fast-track nature. This could involve rental of a lecture hall or other suitable venue for several evenings. A planned story set is told, suitably linking the crafted but full detail stories without interjecting teaching to disrupt the story flow. This could last over several sessions—typically five evenings. It is generally not possible to give an evangelistic invitation unless the venue or other circumstances permit doing so.*
- *Look for other opportunities to provide a brief or lengthy (as need or opportunity permits) fast-track presentation primarily of the evangelism track stories and accompanied by use of Bible teaching pictures (if this is culturally acceptable). Fast-track storying has been used in evangelistic "hit and run" encounters where contact time was relatively short but avoided government or other hostile interference during an opportunity.*

Point of Ministry Storying is also called *Situational Storying*. Point of Ministry stories are one or two appropriate stories which are chosen for the moment and are usually thematic in relationship rather than chronological. These are related to some ministry opportunity in a home or elsewhere, to probe for response, or to initiate a longer storying strategy if there is interest from listeners.

- *Story opportunity when invited to enter a home to pray for a family member or family need. Before offering prayer as requested, take an opportunity to lift up Jesus as the one who opened access to the Father and taught us how to pray. Tell one or more of the stories of Jesus and then pray. Always use this opportunity to offer a return visit to make a traditional Chronological Bible Storying presentation or evangelistic Fast-track presentation for the family, friends and neighbors. The story before prayer might be followed by a longer opportunity to fast-track while waiting for any hospitality or meal offered by the family.*

- *Any life passage rites or events where opportunity is given for teaching or sharing. These opportunities might open at marriages, the birth of children, circumcision rites or other coming of age rites, birthdays, funerals, or memorials. Among the Taureg people a missionary husband and wife were asked to tell stories during a wedding festival. The event proved to be popular and led to other opportunities to tell Bible stories at weddings. In Bangladesh a short-term worker brought a clown suit and made himself available for children's birthday parties. As the performer he had opportunity to tell Bible stories.*
- *National holidays or holy days when some celebration or gathering presents an opportunity to publicly share appropriate Bible stories. This might not be an appropriate time to give an invitation but is an opportunity to offer to return at another time when Bible Storying might be done under different circumstances among those showing interest.*
- *Meetings of service clubs when invited to speak. Bible stories might need to be combined with other stories as appropriate for the occasion and incorporated into a story set with the Bible story(ies) given a prominent place among the other stories. Informal home clubs or other similar gatherings provide additional opportunities, giving opportunity to speak, and telling a story/ies is appropriate or expected.*
- *Bible Storying art display — This concept was used by James H. Taylor III in Taiwan during ministry among students. Students would set up easels with Bible pictures in a public park and stand by each picture. As viewers came by each student would tell the story of his/her picture. Later these pictures were put into books and used by individuals to tell the stories while traveling on trains. Pictures were contextualized for Chinese viewers.*

- *Medical, dental, well baby and eyeglass clinics during patient waiting time. These can be cyclic fast-track presentations offered in repeat cycles as new patients come in. They could also be considered as coupled ministries in home visits to new mothers.*

Coupled Ministries

Coupled Ministries are storying opportunities that are longer than typical Point of Ministry opportunities and are coupled with or made possible in conjunction with a training or ministry program. These programs bring listeners together for longer time frames. The stories and related teaching could be chronological in order, thematic, or mixed according to need.

- *Agricultural training—Where trainees are in residence for several weeks or longer there is time to tell a complete track of stories, repeat them as needed, teach from the stories and give practice storying time for the trainees.*
- *Development projects—Development projects that last longer than a few days give ample opportunity for a complete storying track to be taught. Drilling of wells and other water projects are typical. Use "Water Stories from the Bible".*[57]
- *Relief Projects—During relief projects it is often possible for initial storying to begin and someone to stay on after the relief phase to continue teaching. Grain distribution during famine could provide opportunity to tell stories about the Bread of Life that satisfies spiritual hunger as well as the God who fed hungry people in their time of need. Use Food Stories from the Bible.*
- *Disaster Response—Relief and rebuilding usually lasts over an extended period of time. It is a time of community unity in reconstruction. Good relationships between the disaster team and local people give excellent opportunity for a selected set of stories that offer assurance and hope, as well as point the way to Christ as Savior. Stories could be told at night after the day's work is finished. "Hope Stories from the*

Bible"[58] *were developed for this need.*

- *English as Second Language classes where professional English is taught as a platform and additional teaching offered via Bible Storying. Also ESL where only Bible Storying is used as the primary teaching tool. Gary and Evelyn Harthcock have provided numerous resources for ESL using Bible stories.*[59]
- *Literacy Projects where Bible stories in simplified language could be used for teaching new readers. Readers practice the stories and learn vocabulary from the stories. Written stories should be developed from told story models to facilitate learning. (See Harthcock ESL materials and ESL/EFL Teaching Tips.)*[60]
- *Other ministry projects—Women's sewing classes and sewing projects to earn income offer opportunity to tell Bible stories during rest breaks or as a part of the overall teaching time.*

Other Storying Tools

- *Reversed Chronology—Jesus First, then Genesis. In some circumstances there is reason to begin with the story of Jesus because of listeners' familiarity with it, expectation that it will be told first, or the need to connect early on through engaging listeners in the stories of Jesus. After the Cross and Resurrection, then go back to Genesis and the Old Testament for a review of the Redemption story as beginning discipling, and to give perspective to the story of Jesus.*
- *Bible Storying in Preaching—Bible Storying preaching tracks are either chronological (historical) or topical (thematic). Chronological tracks follow the history timeline of the stories and pick up themes along the way in the context of the timeline. Topical (thematic) tracks are usually organized thematically. Whether they are chronological in organization depends upon the location of the stories, and the logical order needed for telling them.*

- *Integrated Bible Stories as components—There is a growing popularity to incorporate Bible stories into other witness and discipling formats. In recent times users of the Camel Training Manual,*[61] *use a basic Quranic reference to initiate witness. Trainers include Bible stories as well as parables, proverbs, and relevant Scripture passages.*

Another format that is making use of Bible Storying as a component is *Training for Trainers* (T4T) and its several variants which stress immediate evangelistic activity by the trainees. The T4T sessions encourage each participant immediately to begin making use of what he/she have learned which can include telling the Bible stories they have learned.

There is now training for storyers who use Bible Storying as part of their T4T training. It has been aptly called ST4T or Storying Training for Trainers. Several in India are using ST4T for equipping and empowering house church leaders.

Providing an Oral Bible

There is one last Bible-Storying tool or function that has become increasingly important. It is the work of providing *Oral Bibles* to those who cannot read, who have unwritten languages, or who lack access to a translation in their spoken language. The Bible as we know it is a book that is written and available in, not only our language, but in many easy-to-read and understand versions in our language. There are approximately 3,000 significant language groups at present lacking written Scriptures. A large proportion of these are oral communicators who lack the necessary literacy to read and understand the Bible competently.

In the early days of this storyer's experience teaching the Bible stories in various Asian countries, I observed that listeners, after hearing the stories, could recall them and repeat them. Using this little bit of Scripture, many began to witness, disciple, and preach. Others had put the stories into song and would sing them while working in the fields. What was happening? The learned Scripture was a living Oral Bible in their hearts. As the number of stories grew and memory verses were learned as part of the storying sessions, the listeners' Oral Bibles increased in size.

Realizing this was happening, I noted it and began calling the phenomenon their *Oral Bible*. For me it was at first just an observation of what was happening. Then it struck me that with additional planning and additional teaching time the Oral Bibles could be enlarged.

Because in the typical Chronological Bible Storying strategy we were continuing through a basic outline of the Bible story of Redemption, it was providing a chronological framework for adding additional stories as well as completing the Bible story after the evangelism, church planting and discipling story lessons.

So the Oral Bible concept was added as a "shadow strategy" in that it shadowed the major strategies of evangelizing and planting churches. The strategy was never intended to replace a properly translated Bible in listeners' spoken language, nor deny their access to adequate literacy to read and understand their Bibles. For some people groups an Oral Bible is a stop-gap effort to give them a working Bible during their lifetime which can be used just as literates use their Bibles for study, meditation, and teaching. For many others, an Oral Bible may be their only Bible for the foreseeable future.

Some of the language groups are very small and these would typically be overlooked for the larger groups who lack Scriptures. Many of the older listeners have impaired eyesight as well so that an Oral Bible not only hurdles their nonliteracy but also hurdles their physical impairment. While proper Bible translations take years to complete, Oral Bibles can be imparted in much less time.

Proper Bible translations will be needed in the future to preserve the accuracy of God's Word. Bible translators have agreed to work with Bible storyers among selected people groups to provide proper translations for the key stories which are needed to evangelize and disciple. The present *OneStory* partnership is providing the needed cooperative assistance to develop new Bible storyers and new Bible translators through an internship program. For details see the OneStory website.[62] In your browser type in the subject line "OneStory" to see the various participating organization websites.

There is another interesting factor among oral communities. They enjoy learning *en community*, that is, as a gathered group, large or small. I noted in my storying sessions that when a brother or sister was attempting to retell a story and stumbled at some point, members of the group were quick to step in and contribute the missing parts. The story belonged to the community. The community possessed an Oral Bible larger than any one member of the community.

There are problems associated with Oral Bibles. Among many peoples, Bible stories, unless they are exercised often by retelling, tend to fade. Stories also get corrupted by similar cultural stories and beliefs leading to syncretism. So there is a need for corrective storying periodically to refresh the stories and other learned passages.

Because it takes time, much time, to teach a large amount of Scripture to listeners, and even more time to come periodically and to refresh the Scripture, it is good to supplement this strategy with recordings of the stories. Within their community oral learners can listen to the stories over and over, keeping them fresh and corrected. This has led to deliberate strategies to select key Bible stories, to prepare simple trade language versions for teaching to bilingual members of the group. These then translate the stories orally while recording them. Once recorded, the stories can be copied as needed, distributed, or played over the radio.

A recent project to provide evangelistic stories and discipling stories for the *Todos Santos Mam* Mayan people of Guatemala followed just such a plan. Key Bible stories were selected and developed into simple Spanish (because some who helped were partially fluent in basic Spanish). To be sure those who were doing the recording understood the stories accurately, it was necessary to teach about the stories to prevent corruption in translation. Then the stories were recorded. This process is being repeated for many people groups. For some the recordings are a mix of narrated stories and sung stories.

In Asian countries where I worked many of the men and women who came to the story training afterward took their Oral Bibles home with them. A young non-literate Bengali woman told me after such a week, "I'm going to tell the people in my village all the stories I've heard this week." Some of the listeners who were marginally literate told me that after they heard the stories and understood them, they could read the stories in their Bibles. In one extreme case one of my interpreters who was highly literate in both his native Bengali and in English said that now he could read the stories in Bengali and understand them better. You will no doubt continue to hear the Oral Bible term used often. One last thought — you, too, have an Oral Bible. It is the Bible you have in your heart which you can recall and share without having to read it from the book. If you are serious about Bible Storying I can assure you that your Oral Bible is going to grow!

Summary

These Bible Storying tools have the purpose of raising the awareness level for using Bible Storying not only strategically, but creatively. The methods also provide openings whenever the opportunity to tell stories arises. The Bible stories, both individually and in clusters or series, are held to be powerful as God's Word speaks to a variety of ministry needs, as well as an intentional witnessing structure.

The value of any tool box is that it holds a variety of tools which have their greatest effectiveness in doing certain tasks. The wise Bible storyer will be aware of these various storying tools and will develop competence enabling her/him to use them as needed. The bottom line is not the desire to do storying in a variety of ways, but to be good workmen who are skilled and alert to handle the Word of truth any time, any where with almost any opportunity.

Fig. 5 Well Equipped Storying Tool Box

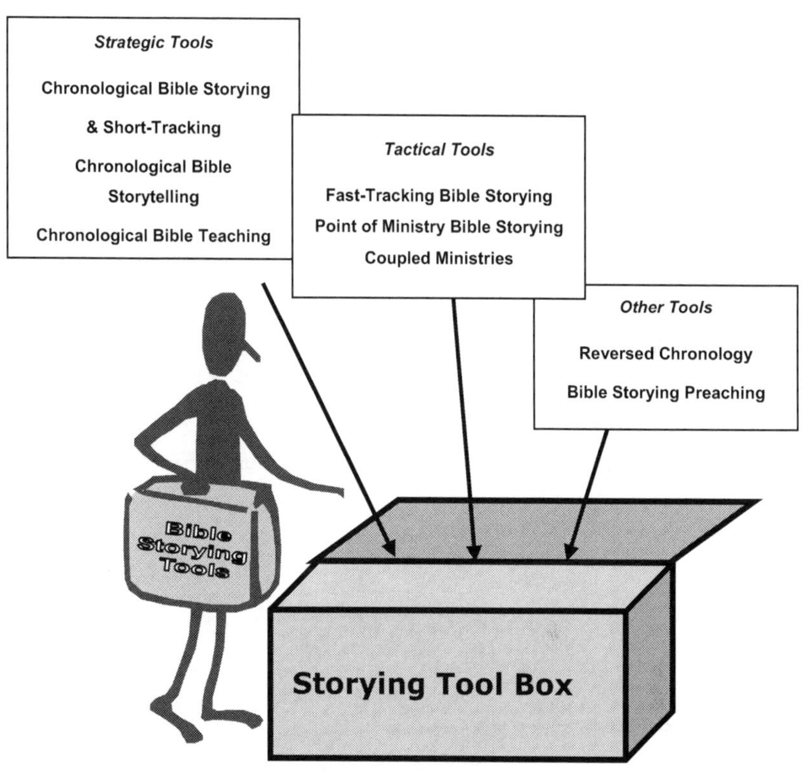

jot

Is your Storying Tool Box well-equipped?

Chapter 19

New Directions for Bible Storying

The concept and practice of Bible Storying continues to evolve. Approaches are being redefined as new needs and opportunities arise. For example, leaders in Bible Storying can view the history and progression of change in the approach. From the initial recovery and popularization of Chronological Bible Teaching for a tribal people in the Philippines, the set of lessons soon contained Bible stories as an integral part. When these story lessons were taken to other peoples, the need for more worldview input led to new story sets that reflected local, spiritual, worldview issues. All of these early chronological teaching approaches were relatively lengthy, comprising thirty-five or more lessons taking many months to complete.

In my area of South Asia, most of the Bible story sets in use were only "oral" in that nothing was written down at that time. The group of oral learner pastors and evangelists learned the stories in the training and discussed how to teach from them. It was later that missionaries asked for copies of the stories and accompanying lessons that some of these were written out in English for sharing.

Soon the need arose for more compact Bible-Storying presentations that could be told in a matter of hours or a day at most. Fast-tracking was born to meet this need. New ministry opportunities called for the appropriate story or stories that were not always chronological in sequence. The home prayer ministries needed an appropriate story or two of Jesus' ministry or teaching. Relief and development projects needed appropriate thematic story sets like *Water Stories from the Bible.*[63] that were still evangelistic, but also served a general purpose of familiarizing listeners with the Bible stories, while entertaining them during the projects.

A current form of fast-tracking the Bible stories or telling a compact presentation from Creation to the stories of Jesus is popularly called *Creation to Christ* or C2C. One variant extends the story set to the End Times as *Creation to Eternity.* If the stories are told as a continuing series without pausing for dialog or teaching then it is fast-tracking. If the storis are paused for dialog then it becomes a compact short-tract story set. Some of these presentations are brief and composed of a condensed summary of the Redemption Story that can be covered in fifteen minutes or less. The prepared storyer can expand the C2C presentation by adding stories and including more story details and dialog to fit the time and opportunity.

While on a return visit to India, this storyer had twelve opportunities among housechurch groups to present Creation to Christ stories that ranged from forty-five minutes to several hours. In at least one place some of the people followed to hear the stories again at the next place. If the listening group is small, teaching pictures can be used to further illustrate the relationship and flow of the stories. It takes initial preparation to select and prepare the stories (or at least decide how and what to tell) and then several presentations to become experienced and competent to do it fluently from memory. There is also a need to be prepared enough to be flexible. The last housechurch group visited was at a time when the adults were away working and the listeners were mostly children. The C2C stories used and how they were told were adjusted for the younger listeners.

For examples of a brif C2C and an expanded C2C, visit www.Bible-Storying.com or contact the author at BibleStorying@ sbcglobal.net

The early Bible Storying strategies targeted whole villages or groups of listeners over many weeks or months. But some situations like patients in a hospital or travelers seated next to you required more compact presentations which could be shared quickly. Missionary Jim McAtee, while serving as chaplain at a Baptist hospital in Indonesia, pioneered the bedside use of a picture-driven story set using a photo album of chronologically arranged Bible pictures. Biblewomen (many of them non-literate) during their home visits used sets of pictures to illustrate the stories and also as their "text" so they could remember what story to tell next. Others who travel and like to witness along the way began to use pocket picture sets as they told the stories to their seat mates.

Due to the lengthy time frame required by the earlier Bible story sets, which sometimes were difficult to complete in a reasonable time, shorter Bible story sets and tracks appeared. Among these were *The Witnessing Kit*[64] from the Philippines and the *Storying Scarf*[65] in West Africa. An even shorter story set was in use in Brazil by Christy Brawner whose story set contained only seven evangelism lessons and eight discipling lessons, all drawn from the Gospel of Matthew.[66]

Among some listeners, because they already knew something about Jesus, or this was their point of interest, storyers began with the story of Jesus first, and then later went back to the Old Testament stories beginning with Genesis. This approach took advantage of the listeners' immediate interest in Jesus. In some areas young Muslim men asked about the *Injil* or Gospel, so missionaries began with the story of Jesus. Among cultural Christians who do not really understand salvation by faith in Jesus, this was a good beginning.

When some Muslim women expressed distaste for Christian teaching, a story set was provided that dealt with their typical life issues, and that contained no structured dialog or discussion as "Christian" teaching. The object was to tell only the stories and allow any discussion to arise from the women listeners. In time many questions would arise and a typical dialog teaching time was possible because the women asked for it. This story set is *Grief Stores from the Bible*.

It was not long before the concept of chronological and nonchronological Bible stories found their way into English as Second Language (ESL) teaching materials like those used by Gary and Evelyn Harthcock, first in Cambodia, and later in Thailand. The Harthcocks produced a number of lesson books with Bible stories in simple English.[67]

Ministry and project specific story sets like *Hope Stories from the Bible*[68] modeled appropriate ministry stories during disaster response. Evangelistic themes are there but the major focus is on God as the source of our hope and providence during time of need. A subtle salvation theme is included though the intent is for a later more in-depth presentation to be made after the door is opened.

Churches in the U.S. asked for help in providing appropriate Bible Storying direction and resources for their short-term mission teams going abroad. *The Short-Term Mission Manual*[69] provided a resource of generic Bible stories which were simplified for use by visiting ministry teams who had to work through interpreters.

Individuals and other teams going on mission trips to target-specific groups like Hindu women asked for very short Bible story sets that could be used during a brief ministry visit. Some of these short sets are only ten-twelve stories which, because of their brevity, are mostly stories of Jesus.

More requests were now coming for listener-specific story sets for use in athletic meets, among Native Americans, or Gypsies. It will take time for story sets like these to be tested and refined in use.

While the original direction for Bible Storying was among the non-literate rural peoples, the concept was finding use in urban areas among literates. Many new options for teaching the stories and discussing them are possible because of literacy and available audiovisual equipment. There are additional opportunities here in the U.S.A. among ministry and recovery groups.

One former Bible Storying trainee in Fort Worth began a story group for women recovering from broken marriages. In Knoxville, Tennessee, the pastor of a church with many in the Deaf congregation found that stories of Bible families provided teaching that spoke to Deaf families. Another pastor, in a South Carolina church where many highly educated employees of a government facility were members, used Bible Storying with the men who expressed their appreciation to the pastor as the stories gave new meaning to the Bible teaching for them.

A growing application is developing for using Bible stories in sharing conversationally and encouraging listeners. Bible stories are included as a key part in the telling of "your story," "my story," and then "God's story." *Lifestory Conversations* by Roy W. Fairchild introduces this concept.[70] A book exploring and applying this concept, *LifeStory Encounters,* is now available.

While it is beyond the scope of this book to explore the approach of formal preaching, there is a growing recovery of *narrative preaching* where Bible stories are told in their entirety rather than just used as a preaching text or illustration. This approach has strong appeal for many postmodern listeners. But the greatest practical need is for modeling and training of nonliterate or low-education pastors in church planting movements. The ones who cannot read and who live and work among people who are oral communicators need to know that God's Word can be preached through story-based sermons that are appropriate for their people. For others who are literate or have low-education, there are typically no Bible study helps or sources of sermon helps available. So it is vital that missionaries and pastors who visit in these areas model for the pastors simple but effective narrative sermons. In my own ministry while still in Asia I had resorted to narrative-based messages to model the preaching and, for those who already had some theological training, to let them see the different response from worshipers when simple relational, narrative sermons were used.

Finally, Bible stories are finding a role as components in other teaching methods like the *CAMEL Training Method.*[71] In addition they are growing in use in *Training for Trainers* (*T4T*).[72]

Some other interesting variations are appearing as well. One is the Visual Story Bible Quilt that was developed by Carla Clements.[73] Carla teaches the stories from the quilt and has provided information and patterns for making your own. In addition, Carla has tied her colorful Visual Quilt to a study of Celebrating God's Appointed Times.

In conclusion, it is evident that a development or discovery process is continuing. This does not negate the original concept of the role of chronologically told Bible stories beginning with Creation. But for those who express interest in a different approach or who are literate and can read the Bible, the options to vary the method work well.

It is still necessary for listeners to understand their sinful nature and helplessness to save themselves from God's wrath in judgment of unforgiven sin. The Old Testament stories provide the perspective for Jesus as Savior. But we are not locked into a rigid structure of Bible Storying that says, *You must do it this way*.

Instead, we are free to explore and learn God's Word as both story and other passages so that, when the need arises or opportunity presents, we will be ready to share the Word with listeners. There may be need and opportunity to teach from the stories as well. But we must be sure to TELL the stories! People will remember the stories, especially those who live in an oral world or who lack the Bible in their own language. Your use of Bible Storying will fit your own ministry pattern and opportunities. Be familiar with all the options—Bible Storying Tools—and choose what is best for your listeners whether literate or not.

Chapter 20
Common Problems, Q & A

In the following pages are shared some of the most commonly asked questions and problems that Bible storyers have encountered over the years. Many of the questions, as well as the answers, have come from my own personal experience with Bible Storying beginning in early 1988, through my retirement from the Asia Pacific Region in 2003, and subsequent two years of consulting on Bible Storying projects in Central and South America. I am greatly indebted to many storyers who have written me over the years sharing their situations and asking for advice and counsel on how to correct their problems related to local use of Bible Storying. The list of questions is by no means exhaustive. I do not suggest that my answers are always the best or even that I always have a satisfactory answer to some problem not listed here.

The *Bible Storying* newsletter[74] has been one way of addressing common questions related to Bible Storying since its beginning in 1994. Back issues of the newsletter share and answer many of these problems. In more recent years the questions continue to come via the Internet.

I am always interested to learn of these questions because as a trainer it is one way that I can stay current on the practice of Bible Storying around the world. In addition, I may know of someone who has had the same or a similar question or problem and can refer the question for his/her advice.

In the beginning, those of us who pioneered in developing the concepts and methodology of Bible Storying possessed little experience and few guidelines to help us. We encountered difficulties and had to seek solutions that worked for us. Much of the present-day Bible Storying methodology owes its existence to those early difficulties and how we found ways to make Bible Storying work in practical and reproducible ways. I would, however, be remiss if not also mentioning that the Lord has been gracious to answer prayers and to guide the development of the methodology and solutions to any difficulties we encountered in telling The

Greatest Story of our God and Savior Jesus.

The most commonly asked question is: "Where can I get a copy of these Bible stories to tell?" I am always tempted to say: "Look in the Bible, that's where I got mine!" But that is not really the question. So the number one question we seek to answer in Bible Storying training is how to decide which Bible stories to tell related to our teaching objectives and informed by local worldview issues. But other questions are real and are asked often. Here are some common questions.

Q: *If the typical Bible story takes only a few minutes to tell, how do you fill up the time?*

A: The Bible Storying Session with its suggested pre-story and post-story learning activities will typically fill the time and then some. The idea is not to fill the time, but to prepare listeners for the story, tell the story, and then give opportunity for listeners *en community* to discuss and apply the story teaching. Oral learners do have a fatigue point at which learning slows down. The astute Bible storyer watches for this and adjusts the session accordingly.

Q: *What if the listeners are too shy or ashamed to respond to my pre-story or post-story Dialog time?*

A: This happens for various reasons. In the beginning the concept of being asked a question and given an opportunity to respond may be a new thing. Give the listeners time and keep the questions very conversational. In some cultures there is fear of shame if giving the wrong answer or worse, not knowing the answer. Some actually believe that it brings shame on the storyer if listeners can't answer the questions. One group of women in Africa responded, "No one ever asked our opinion before."

In some West African cultures the men's groups may have a *delegué* who is the designated spokesman. If no response is forthcoming, just introduce the stories, tell them, and leave listeners to ponder the stories. The Holy Spirit will raise questions in their hearts and in time they will want to talk about the stories.

Q: *I notice in the set of Bible Storying lessons someone gave me there are many questions to ask after the story.*

How can non-literate listeners remember all these questions to ask after they tell the stories?

A: They can't. Initially the written story sets were prepared for missionaries to give them a resource for preparing their own Bible Storying Session. If part of the objective is to equip listeners in turn to tell the stories and lead their listeners to discuss the stories, then a simpler, limited set of stock questions works better. In Bangladesh, Ethiopia, and other countries a limited list of the same questions is used for each story. (See resources for this in "Bible Storying Helps".)

Q: *What if I tell all my stories and give an invitation and no one responds to believe on Jesus as Savior?*

A: First, know how people in the various cultures respond to questions like this. In some cases listeners will begin responding even before such an invitation is given. But where there appears to be no response, the storyer has several options. One is to go back through the Core Bible Stories a second time. (Don't make any explanation why this is being done.) The listeners might need this time to continue reflecting on the stories and the implications for their lives. Also this gives those joining late an opportunity to hear all the stories.

Second, move on to another listener group, perhaps nearby, and begin with them. Stay in touch with the first group so as questions begin to arise regarding the stories you can help them to discuss the stories. I have found that sometimes individuals in a listener group may make a decision for Jesus but out of fear of persecution not reveal it until later.

Q: *What if when I finish all my stories and give an invitation only one or two listeners respond?*

A: Most oral learners live in communal societies where it is not good to get out of line — that is, to be different from the others. So, if it is possible, take those listeners aside and test their decisions, pray with them, explain what it means to believe on Jesus as Savior, but tell them to keep their peace until others have made the same decision. Review the basic stories to give additional time and opportunity to draw the net for the others. A decision to respond may need time to develop as a community consensus or for a leader to respond first. Among some women it has been necessary to keep their response a quiet or secret response until they are led to make it known.

Q: *What if some of the listeners who already know something about the Bible or Jesus say they want to believe on him before reaching the last stories?*

A: In the early days of Bible Storying one of the storyers from the Philippines said that he was only on story thirty-two out of fifty-four stories when this happened. The first time he told the person to wait that he hadn't finished his stories! We suggest again taking those listeners aside, privately witnessing to them, and testing their decision. Ask them to be patient until the others in the group are able to believe like they do.

Q: *How do you begin Bible Storying in a new place? Do you just go someplace, gather some people, and begin telling the stories?*

A: In order to establish the best relationship with leaders or influential persons in a community, it is always best to seek permission to tell the stories. It is even better if you are asked or invited to tell the stories. In many of my training sessions done in publicly accessible places, listeners who were from other villages asked that someone come and tell their people these same stories. If denied permission but shown some hospitality, look for an opportunity to share one or two stories as "entertainment" and leave it with the listeners. Perhaps they will invite you back to tell more stories. Tell a fast-track story to test for responsiveness.

Q: *When I begin a new storying group many people come out of curiosity. But after a few stories, some of the people stop coming. What should I do?*

A: This often happens. It has happened to me. One thing I learned is not to stop, for those who are not present are still "listening," but are just not present. Those who do not attend will ask those who did what the story was. This is good as it gives opportunity for listeners to retell the story.

I have found that the patriarch "family" stories are very interesting to listeners. Some of the more "theological" stories and discourses are less interesting unless related to some cultural aspect. When initial attendance has declined, it usually picks up again with the stories of Jesus. Also, stories that are similar to their culture or that provide answers to questions their worldview does not provide will draw attention and interest.

Q: *My Bible Storying sessions are more like a circus than a proper teaching session. How can I help the listeners to treat these stories seriously?*

A: One of the primary reasons for telling the Bible stories in public settings is to make them available to the group of listeners at large. The storying session is not a worship service, it is a learning time. Oral learners are often noisy when learning. Do not be distracted by their lack of "learning etiquette."

A good session among oral learners will provide lots of opportunity for their participation in the learning by retelling stories (with other listeners helping them) and in having the group to repeat teaching charts like *The Characteristics of God,* the *Ten Commandments,* or even a memory verse. I had to get used to having women listeners chatting among themselves while I told the stories. I thought they weren't listening. But they were — as individuals and as a group.

Q: *The women I work with don't want any "Christian" teaching? How can I teach the Storying Sessions to them?*

A: This is common among some of the conservative Muslim groups. When this was initially encountered, I found that the problem was not in *telling* the story but in *teaching* from the story which was viewed as "Christian" preaching. This led to *Grief Stories from the Bible* model in which stories of Bible women and their misfortunes were told but without any teaching. The stories provoked discussion and over several stories acceptance grew and relationship and trust developed so that listeners began to ask questions or make comments which led to conversational dialog in which teaching could take place.

Q: *I can't always go to my listeners at the appointed time to tell the new stories. If I don't go then the next time I do go there are fewer listeners gathered. What can I do?*

A: There are three suggestions I'd make. One is to team teach so that two (or more) share in teaching. If one cannot be present, then the other can tell the new story. A suggestion is to begin training a helper among the listeners who can review the previous stories and memory verses in your absence. A suggestion is to record the stories and have someone among the listeners play the new story. When there is a break in the stories, for whatever reason, it is always good to review previous stories before continuing with a new story.

Q: *What should I do if my listeners cannot retell the Bible story?*

A: First, tell the story again and ask again for a retelling. If not, suggest that someone begin the story and go as far as he/she is able. Then another can add to the story as far as he/she is able. Continue to encourage the group of listeners to tell the story as best they can. When they finish, you tell it again. Then ask again if one of the listeners can now tell the story. Do not scold or belittle failure.

Do not be embarrassed to retell a story as oral learners usually enjoy repetition, especially if it is done in a way in which they enjoy participating. In Bolivia a storying group had told the stories in Spanish. They decided to try the stories in the Quechua language. One non-literate woman who had not previously participated, listened to the group struggle with the story in their native but little used Quechua language as they sought to find the words and right expressions. Now the non-literate woman began to grasp and understand the story as it was in her language. Suddenly she spoke up and began to tell the story fluently in her native Quechua. One elder leader I knew among the *Kui* people in India never would retell a story in front of me. But I learned later that when his pastor did not come one Sunday that he ran to get a set of pictures and told the Bible stories to the worshipers.

Q: *What do I do after my listeners profess their faith in Jesus as Savior?*

A: Depending on circumstances it may be well to quickly review the key Bible stories leading to salvation as an initial discipling to affirm their decisions. Without announcing that you are beginning a new story track simply pick up the stories of the New Testament church after Jesus ascended into heaven. The Acts stories should begin to provide a model for the listeners who are now believers. I always liked to hear the listeners ask, "Why haven't we been baptized? We believe like those people!" Or, "Now that we are Christians what should we do?"

Q: *Where I tell the Bible stories there are many cultural Christians who want to have a worship service. What should I do? Should we pray and sing songs before telling the stories?*

A: Unless people are born again they are not really ready to worship. It is not uncommon for many oral learners to look for some ritual to follow as their native religions often prescribe certain rituals.

I suggest that the storyer pray at home before the session, and if prayer is used, that it be a short prayer for God to bless the story from His Word. Where the listeners are nominal Christians they may want to sing their traditional worship songs. This is not a problem unless it keeps non-believers away. Among many Hindus I found that singing actually drew attention and brought listeners. The Bible Storying Session is a teaching session and not a worship service. But if the people want to begin singing songs, especially toward the stories of Jesus, this may be helpful when the time comes to begin worship.

Q: *I want to use Bible Storying but I have only six months or less before I have to leave for the U.S. What should I do?*

A: You may not be able to plant a church in the limited time you have but you can use it to cover key Bible stories leading to salvation. You will need to decide how many storying sessions you can count on and then select your stories accordingly. If at all possible train someone to team story with you to continue the group on to church. Sadly, some storyers begin sessions without planning ahead to their Stateside Assignment time. There are many possibilities for shorter storying tracks or for using clusters of several stories during each session if the listeners can digest that many new stories.

Q: *I have a hard time myself remembering all those Bible stories. What can I do to work around this?*

A: Welcome to the world of oral learners where we literate Westerners are the disadvantaged! In many places there is no problem with having your open Bible or even a notebook of prepared stories as long as you properly relate the stories to the Bible. There was a time when I struggled with this and even posted notes on the backside of teaching pictures to remind me of the stories. But in time as I told the same stories over and over I learned the stories.

Two secrets relate to this problem of remembering stories. One is to remember that good storytellers do not repeat a memorized story but instead recreate the story as they tell it. (Of course, we want to do this as accurately as possible.) The other is that I learned to position myself in the stories so that I was telling what I was seeing and hearing as the story happened all about me. For me then the story was not being recalled from my memory but being experienced as I told it. This did not come right away. We told the same stories week-after-week and sometimes several times in one day. Be patient. You will own the stories in due time.

Professional storyteller John Walsh suggests that you use body motions and gestures to visualize the story. In this way you are teaching your body the story as well as your mind. Then your body can help your mind to tell the stories!

Q: *I keep finding new worldview issues among my listeners. Sometimes I realize that the story I have chosen is not the best one to challenge their worldview.*

A: This happens as you tell the stories. You will never know all there is to know about your listeners' worldview. Some of it they won't tell you as an outsider but it may come out in their reaction to stories or discussion of the stories. I learned of the problem with the *David and Bathsheba* story, and the *Samaritan Woman* story and others when I told them and did not get the response I expected. Worldview and culture of the listeners evoked a different response to which I needed to respond. In general it takes at least three times through a story set for it to settle down after making any needed story adjustments to accommodate the new worldview issues that come to light.

Q: *What if I have both oral learners and literates among my listeners? To whom do I teach?*

A: Story to the oral learners and do not allow the literate listeners to dominate the sessions. Encouraging the oral learners to retell the stories may give them an edge over the literates. Also do not allow children who are very keen listeners and eager to tell the stories to take the session away from the adults.

Q: *What if I find that my listeners are forgetting the stories I have told or they are changing the stories so that sometimes the stories are really corrupted?*

A: Forgetting the stories is what we call *fading*. It is like the memory in a computer that must be refreshed from time to time. Frequent exercising of stories by recalling them, telling them, or sometimes relating stories to certain communal events can help. Look for someone in the community who is a "keeper of stories" and train the person to keep the stories alive.

Restructuring of stories happens when the people do not understand the story and so misinterpret it, they don't like the story and so fix it, or the story is in some way close to one of their myths and there is confusion or mixing of the two. One of the best defenses against restructuring is to carefully link or to relate each story to the preceding and following stories so that it is locked in. If necessary, take time to differentiate between their story and the Bible story, and talk about the differences.

I am sure that you, too, will have questions as you begin your own Bible Storying strategy or ministry. Send them to Biblestorying@sbcglobal.net or Biblestorying@iname.com and I'll try to find an answer for you or refer you to someone who has expressed a similar question or problem.

Chapter 21

Resources for Bible Storying

Thomas E. Boomershine, *Story Journey: An Invitation to the Gospel as Storytelling* (Nashville: Abingdon, 1988). Paper

> This is a basic text on biblical storytelling. Boomershine says the purpose of the book is to recover the gospel as storytelling. The only way to do this is to learn to tell (Bible) stories. The author uses several parables as examples for telling the Bible stories. This text can be read over and over for inspiration.

Richard L. Pratt, Jr., *He Gave Us Stories: the Bible Student's Guide to Interpreting Old Testament Narratives* (New Jersey, Presbyterian & Reformed Publishing Company, 1990). Paper.

> In Part II: *Investigating Old Testament Narratives* Pratt gives a review of studying Old Testament characters, scene depiction, writers and their audiences, and an overview of Old Testament narratives. The text is not about Bible Storying as such but is a helpful study of understanding Old Testament narratives so that they can be communicated effectively as stories.

Jacob A. Loewen, *Culture and Human Values: Cultural Intervention in Anthropological Perspective* (South Pasadena, CA: William Carey Library, 1975) Paper.

> The chapter on "*Bible Stories: Message and Matrix*" is at once one of the best mini-case studies of using Bible Storying among an indigenous people, a historical account of an early use of Bible story lessons brought to Panama, and used among the Choco people. I count this one chapter as "must" reading. The book is out of print so look for it in school libraries.

Walter J. Ong, *Orality & Literacy: The Technologizing of the Word* (London & New York: Routledge, 1988) Paper.

> The key book setting forth the differences between literates and non-literates. Chapters 3 and 6 give

special attention to the characteristics of people living in oral or secondary oral cultures. This book, though technical, is essential in justifying the use of storytelling strategies in reaching oral people. This is a scholarly work on the basics of orality and is not easy reading for the casual reader.

Tex Sample, *Ministry in an Oral Culture: Living with Will Rogers, Uncle Remus and Minnie Pearl* (Louisville, KY: Westminster/ John Knox, 1994). Paper.

Sample gives a simpler, more practical, and more entertaining description of the dynamics that Ong writes about. But Sample's focus is just on the U. S.A. He also quotes a few "hard living people" saying vulgar things. But his book is a useful introduction to orality in the U. S. If you are planning a ministry in the U. S.A., don't miss this book.

Herbert V. Klem, *Oral Communication of the Scripture: Insights from African Oral Art* (Pasadena, CA: William Carey Library, 1982).

This book is out of print. If you can find a copy it is an excellent read on orality from an African perspective with comparison between West Africa and 1st century Palestine. From a missiological perspective the author presents the urgent need to communicate the Scriptures to the non-literate majority of the world's population.

Trevor McIlwain, *Building on Firm Foundations* (Sanford, FL: New Tribes Mission, 1987) Paper.

Of the nine volumes the most useful to the student of Bible Storying are volumes 1 & 2 which cover the background of chronological-Bible teaching and McIlwain's experience, findings, and practicum of addressing the need of a people unprepared for the Gospel. The stress is on building a firm foundation through a chronological teaching of Bible truths in the Old Testament before presenting the teachings from the Gospels. Volume 1 is *Guidelines for Evangelism and Teaching Believers*. Volume 2 has an excellent introduction to evangelistic chronological teaching followed by McIlwain's Old Testament expositional lessons.

Tom A. Steffen, *Passing the Baton: Church Planting That Empowers* (La Habra, CA: Center for Organizational & Ministry Development, 1993) Paper.

> Steffen's basic argument is to teach and train to empower national leadership in preparation for missionary exit. He is a former New Tribes missionary who began with Chronological- Bible Teaching lessons among a tribal group in the Philippines and came to realize the value of teaching via Bible stories which his listeners could understand and recall.

Tom A. Steffen, *Reconnecting God's Story to Ministry: Crosscultural Storytelling at Home and Abroad* (La Habra: Center for Organizational & Ministry Development, 1996) Paper.

> Steffen says, "I wrote this book primarily to help readers recapture the most natural, universal and effective means of evangelism-discipleship that exists—storytelling." The author uses slightly different vocabulary to cover the basics of understanding the storylands, the storybook, the storyline and smithing (*sic*) the story for telling.

David J. Hesselgrave, *Communicating Christ Cross-Culturally: An Introduction to Missionary Communication*, 2nd ed. (Grand Rapids, MI: Zondervan, 1991) Paper.

> Effective Bible Storying relies on good understanding of the culture and worldview of the listeners. Chapters on various worldview perspectives are helpful in understanding the basics of cross-cultural communication using Bible stories. (Chap. 11-16 are especially helpful.

Gailyn Van Rheenen, *Communicating Christ in Animistic Contexts* (Grand Rapids, MI: Baker Book House, 1991) Paper.

> The main divisions are Understanding Animism, Thinking Theologically in Animistic Contexts, and Analyzing Animistic Practices and Powers. His

conclusion deals with sin and salvation in Christianity and Animism. Much of the text relates well to Bible Storying in folk-religion contexts.

Paul G. Hiebert, *Anthropological Insights for Missionaries* (Grand Rapids, MI: Baker Book House, 1985). Paper.

This book is a helpful text for understanding the basics of culture and worldview principles. Students should check references in the Index.

Don Richardson, *Eternity in Their Hearts* (Ventura, CA: Regal Books, 1981). Paper.

This is not a book about Bible Storying but about *redemptive analogies* as history and happenings in a people's culture that can predispose them to an openness toward Christianity. Many Bible stories resonate with various redemptive analogies so the Bible storyer is wise to be alert to discover them.

James P. Spradley, *The Ethnographic Interview* (New York, NY: Holt, Rinehart & Winston, 1979). Paper.

Spradley's work is a standard text on conducting interviews to gain cultural and worldview knowledge. Formerly this information was known as an "Ethnography."

Vincent J. Donovan, *Christianity Rediscovered* (Maryknoll, NY: Orbis Books, 1978). Paper.

Donovan was a Catholic missioner among the Maasai in Tanzania who discovered the power of Bible stories in helping the people to understand the Gospel and church.

N. T. Wright, *Christian Origins and the Question of God, vol. 1, The New Testament and the People of God* (Minneapolis, MN: Fortress, 1992).

This text provides an important biblical rationale for narrative approaches to Christian witness. Wright's discussions of worldview and storytelling on pages 31-46, 65-69, 77-80, and 121-144 are basic. The book is an expensive text. Look for it in a library.

In addition look for resources on the following websites:

http://www.CBstorying.com

http://www.oralbible.com

http://www.christianstorytelling.com/ (John Walsh, Christian storyteller)

http://www.stevedenning.com/learn.htm (Storytelling)

http://www.eldrbarry.net/mous/bibl/narr.htm (Discerning Biblical Story Structures)

http://www.eldrbarry.net/ (The Art of Storytelling)

http://www.timsheppard.co.uk/story/tellinglinks.html (Storytelling Links for Storytellers)

http://www.chronologicalbible.org/ (Chronological Scripture resources)

http://www.nobs.org/ (Network of Biblical Storytellers)

http://www.ijfm.org/archives.htm (International Journal of Frontier Missions, in the Google space type "Bible Storying" for archive articles on Bible Storying)

http://www.siutraining.org/ (Scriptures In Use training and resources for storying to semiliterates. Click on *Training* or *Resources*.)

www.Bible-Stroying.com

On any of the search engines enter the subject: "Chronological Bible Storying," or "Bible Storying" to see more resources and reports of using Bible Storying among various people groups.

Chapter 22

Bible Storying Helps

The Bible Storying Helps are some additional lists of items which may be helpful to the beginning storyer in developing an Evangelism Track and for those who are interested in developing storying tracks beyond the basic Evangelism Track. The lists are representative and should only be used for study and resources for developing your own lists of Bible truths to emphasize with sensitivity to your listeners' spiritual needs.

Basic Bible Truth Sample Lists

Church Planting Track

1. Believers receive the Holy Spirit when they profess their faith in Jesus. The Holy Spirit convicts of sin in the believers' lives and strengthens their faith.
2. Those who believe on Jesus as Savior are to be baptized.
3. Believers are to gather into a community of faith— to praise God in worship together regularly as a church.
4. Believers are to live in a fellowship of harmony and peace with one another.
5. Believers are to give testimony of their faith in Christ and live a life that is a good testimony to others who are not believers.
6. Believers are to continue receiving teaching from God's Word.
7. Believers are to observe the Lord's Supper in an orderly and worshipful manner to remember Jesus' death for their sins.
8. Believers are to pray for one another.
9. Believers are to minister to the needs of believers in the church.
10. Believers are to minister to needs of those outside the church, praying for them in the name of Jesus, and making use of the resources God gives the church.

11. Believers are, with the guidance of the Holy Spirit, to appoint leaders.
12. Believers are to evangelize others as led by the Holy Spirit.
13. Believers are to be good stewards of their possessions, giving a tithe (or appropriate portion) as an offering.
14. Believers may suffer persecution because of their faith in Jesus.

Characterization (Discipling) Track

1. Disciples are to love the Lord their God with all their hearts, with all their souls, and with all their minds.
2. Disciples show their love to God and Jesus by obeying their commandments.
3. Disciples are to love not only their neighbors, but also their enemies.
4. Disciples are to do unto others as they would have others do unto them.
5. Disciples are to be humble, not seeking self-gain, but have servants' hearts, serving one another.
6. Disciples are to forgive one another's sins (offenses).
7. Disciples are to admonish one another with all wisdom, warning those who fall into sin and restoring them.
8. Disciples are to honor their parents, love and respect their spouses, and be good parents for their children.
9. Disciples are to be sober.
10. Disciples are to live as children of light, shunning all forms of evil—dishonesty, immorality, drunkenness, quarreling, backbiting, impurity, idolatry, jealously and envy, and dissension — living a life that is pleasing to God and a good testimony before others by their godly lives.
11. Disciples are to be repenting, confessing their sins, and asking the Lord's forgiveness.

12. Disciples are to be peacemakers, exhibiting the fruit of the Spirit — love, joy, patience, kindness, goodness, faithfulness, gentleness, and self-control.
13. Disciples must stand firm when persecution comes, persevering with faith in Jesus and filled with the Holy Spirit.
14. Disciples are to make disciples of others, baptizing them, and teaching them to obey all things the Lord commanded.
15. Disciples are to be constant in prayer and intercession for others.
16. Disciples are to be one in hearts, spirits, and faith.
17. Disciples are to grow in the knowledge of the Son of God and become mature, having the same mind as that of Christ, abiding in Christ in order to bear much fruit.
18. Disciples are to be good stewards of the gifts of the Holy Spirit, using them to honor God and building up the community of faith.
19. Disciples are to be thankful and cheerful.
20. Disciples are to be generous in giving to the Lord and in giving toward the needs of others.
21. Disciples are to be faithful in worship, not forsaking the assembling of the community of faith.
22. Disciples are to be bold in witnessing.
23. Disciples are to be law abiding citizens, honoring their rulers.
24. Disciples must continue to study God's Word like good workmen, meditating upon it, and rightly dividing the Word of truth.
25. Disciples must be careful in observing the Lord's Supper, examining and judging themselves, recognizing the body of Christ before eating the bread and drinking the cup.
26. Disciples are to be at work, watching for the Lord's Return.

Note: This list is neither definitive nor exhaustive but is representative of the biblical truths describing the disciple's life. For your people pick out the critical and immediately needed truths to stabilize new believers in their faith, characterize them in Christ and their emerging community of faith, and add any needed truths not listed here.

End Times Track

1. Jesus promised to return for his followers after preparing a place for them.
2. Jesus will return at a time known only by the Father.
3. Jesus will return in power and with his mighty angels.
4. Jesus will return as judge of the living and the dead—to judge unbelievers according to their works recorded in the book of life to reward believers according to their works done in obedience and in the name of Jesus.
5. Jesus warned his followers to be vigilant, prayerful and working, awaiting his Return.
6. Jesus warned his followers to be good stewards of that which he gave them and for which he will demand an accounting.
7. Jesus warned of the danger of falling away in the end times.
8. Jesus will return as the glorified Lamb, the one worthy to receive glory, honor, and power.
9. The angels will harvest the souls of people at the end of the age and will gather the elect from the four corners of the earth.
10. Jesus will defeat Satan and his demons and eternally punish them.
11. Jesus warned that he disciplines those whom he loves.
12. Jesus will clothe believers with his righteousness.
13. A new heaven and a new earth will be prepared to replace the present ones which have passed away.
14. God himself will again dwell among men and they will be his people.

15. All death and mourning, crying or pain will pass away, and God will wipe every tear from the eyes.

Note: *This is a resource list. You will need to limit and prioritize it, reword it or expand it as needed for your people.*

Church-Planting Resource Story List

1. Jesus kept his promise to send the Holy Spirit to the believers. (Jn. 14:15-16, 26; Ac. 2:4; 10:45,47)
2. The believers gathered on a regular basis for prayer. (Ac. 1:12-14; 2:46; 5:12; 16:13-15)
3. The believers began to testify of their faith in Jesus in Jerusalem where they lived. (Ac. 2:14-41; 4:33)
4. Those who believed in Jesus were baptized and God added them to the church. (Mt. 28:19; Ac. 2:38-41; 8:26-39; 10:23-48; 16:13-34)
5. The believers gathered to be taught by the apostles who followed the pattern set by Jesus. (Ac. 2:42; Mt. 5:1-12; Mk. 4:1-2, 10, 34; Lk. 11:1-4; 2Ti. 2:2; Jas. 1:23)
6. The believers gathered in fellowship. (Ac. 2:42, 46; Ps. 1; Mal. 3:16; Ro. 1:12; Php. 1:3; Ac. 16:14-15, 40)
7. The church broke bread together. (Lk. 22:14-20; Ac. 2:46; 1Co. 11:17-34)
8. The believers gathered in the temple courts for worship. (Ac. 2:46; Ps. 27:4; 84:10: 122:1; Heb. 10:25; 12:28)
9. The believers shared with one another and provided for the needs of the church in their giving. (Ac. 2:45; Mk. 7:11-13; Lk. 19:1-8; Jn. 6:1-13; Php. 4:14-19)
10. The believers ministered to those in need in the name of Jesus, trusting Jesus to help them minister. (Ac. 3:1-10; 5:12-16; Mt. 10:1; Mk. 6:7)
11. The believers learned the power of prayer. (Ac. 4:1-26, 31; 12:1-5)
12. The Holy Spirit disciplined believers who sinned. (Ac. 5:1-11; 8:9-24)
13. The believers organized to care for the needs of the

neglected and helpless—the first deacons. (Ac. 6:1-7)

14. The believers began to suffer persecution because of their faith in Jesus, even to the point of death. (Ac. 5:17-41; 6:11-13; 7:54-60; 8:1; Mt. 5:10-12)
15. The believers began to send out evangelists to other places to tell about Jesus. As a result new groups were formed. (Ac. 8:4-7; 14-17, 25; 13:1-5)
16. The believers learned that God's Word was for all people and before God was no distinction as to race. (Ac. 10:1-48; 11:19-23; 13:48; Gal. 3:28)
17. God continued to call out new leaders—even those who initially were against Jesus and persecuted his followers. (Ac. 7:58; 8:1a; 9:1-28)
18. God sent his angels to prepare people for the gospel and gave his Holy Spirit to them when they believed and were baptized. (Ac. 10:1-48)
19. The believers had become one body in Christ. There was unity in their faith, in their worship, in their ministry, and in their testimonies. (Ac. 4:32; Rom. 12:5; 1Co. 1:10; 10:17; Eph. 4:1-5, 13
20. The believers were now God's people. (Ex. 19:5-6; Eph. 5:29-30; 1Pe. 2:9-10)
21. The church had no building but met in homes of the believers. (Ac. 2:46; 12:12; Mt. 18:20; 28:20; 1Co. 3:16; Eph. 2:19-22; 1Pe. 2:5)
22. The church lived in fear of the Lord. (Ac. 9:31; Jn. 14:23-24; Ps. 34:9; Pr. 9:10; Isa. 11:3; Rev. 14:7)

Note: *Some of these stories which are needed to characterize the New Testament church will need to be synthesized, that is, put into a narrative from a base reference and amplified from the additional story references from Acts and other books. Some of the passages have been broken up to allow for emphasis on specific characteristics. Some are repeated as needed. It is possible to combine some of the stories to shorten the story list. Select those themes most applicable to local need.*

Common Spiritual, Social and Other Barriers to the Gospel

1. Ignorance: Of Spiritual Truth: unintentional—have never heard, no access to Scripture.
2. Agnosticism: Intentional doubting, denial, or lack of interest in spiritual truth.
3. Atheism: Intentional anti-God, anti-Christian belief, professing to be a-religious, secularist. (Also some atheistic cultural Christian lifestyle and New Age spiritual beliefs.)
4. Apathy:
   - Resignation to one's *fate* in life: Sex—specially as a woman in major religions, birth defects, lingering or terminal illness, caste, and family religion.
   - Moral insensitivity: Prostitution, gambling, drunkenness and drugs, theft and piracy, murder.
   - Worldliness: Hedonism and good life; materialism: success, prosperity cult.
5. Social Conventions That May Offend: Marrying close relatives or not, unchaperoned relations between men and women who are not married, and sensitivity to issues in biblical stories that are not in keeping with local social practice.
6. Cultural Traditions: Those conflicting with the teachings in God's Word and not consistent with Christian living; national identity and culture equated with prevalent religion, other practices like polygamy, certain rites of passage, shame vs. guilt cultures, cultures that practice nonforgiveness, or revenge to defend family honor. Also traditions related to national and religious leaders where stories depict them in a bad light.
7. Former Religious Beliefs and Practices Carried Over to Christianity: Syncretism resulting from superstition, idol worship, amulets, charms, fetishes, Maryolatry, earth goddess, village deities, festivals and feasts related to local holy days, pilgrimages, rituals, reliance on ecstatic trances and utterances in worship, and false prophets.
8. Other Religious Teachings: Christian "Judaizers," cults that

teach that another truth source besides the Bible is needed or insist on unbiblical practices or works.

9. Nominalism: Degenerate faith of believers, Christians-by-birth, self-righteous "Pharisee-ism" of super-Christians, spiritual laziness, or hardness of heart by those who profess Christianity.
10. Fear of Persecution: Ridicule, shame and loss of face, family and peer pressure to conform, threat of physical harm whether real or imagined, and threat of death.
11. Fear of Losing Material and Social Benefits: Loss of schooling benefits for children, family medical benefits, burial places, relief aid in times of need or disaster, denial to use wells, loss or crops of communal help in agriculture, and damage to family property or loss of land.
12. Fear of Disturbing Community Harmony: Consequences to family and neighbors, becoming a divided society along religious lines, and problems at festival times.
13. Fear of Disturbing Spirit World: Threat of curses and other consequences to self and family from vengeful spirits, and concern for care and fate of community ancestral spirits, and filial duties to departed parents.
14. Demon Possession, Involvement with Satanic Rituals, Magic, Other Practices Invoking the Spirit World for Power, Mediums, Shamans & Witchdoctors.
15. Alcoholism or Use of Hallucigenic Substances to Enhance Worship (*peyote* and *yagé* use)
16. Misinformation & Biases About Christianity: False teachings and popular misconceptions about Christianity and the Bible, rumors and hearsay about Christians.
17. Christianity Is a "Western" Religion and Equated With Western (American) Imperialism.
18. Vocabulary & Theological Truths There Is Strong Disagreement With: "Israelite," Jesus as "Son of God" (Muslims), teachings about "Mary", other words or teachings that because of strong disagreement provoke anger and hinder listening and acceptance).

19. Vocabulary & Theological Terms Commonly Misused by Others: Prayer, "Lord," baptism, salvation, paradise — words that others use that have a very different meaning from the evangelical Christian use of the word.
20. Gaps In Spiritual Knowledge, Unanswered Spiritual World-view Questions and Issues.
21. Lack of Scriptures In Target Language (Mother Tongue) or Only In Regional Trade Language.
22. Borrowed Religious Words From Prevailing Religion Used In Translation of Bible: Words which are borrowed from Buddhism and Islam. Also local laws about Christians using borrowed and restricted religious words.
23. Literacy Competency of People: Non-literates and functional non-literates, those with low educational level who may understand simplified oral presentations better than by reading.
24. Inappropriate or Unfamiliar Literate Teaching Methodology Among Oral Communicators.
25. Teaching Methodology That Is Poorly Organized: Too Heavily Content-Oriented (too much information), Presented Too Quickly (without adequate discussion and digestion time for listeners), or Limited In Thoroughness (to deal with stubborn worldview issues, misunderstanding or lack of leading commitment to appropriate response.)
26. Gatekeepers Who Control Access to a People or Influence Their Decisions to Change or Adapt New Ways: Governments and religious leaders, others seeking to conserve the old ways.
27. Weather and Agricultural Seasons That Limit Access to a People or Impose Time Limits On Access.
28. Religious Festivals and Other Community Events That Distract and Preoccupy People.
29. Cultural Expectations on When, Where and by Whom Truth (true stories) May be Taught.
30. Historical Events Like the Crusades, Colonial Times, War, or Civil Religious Strife.

31. Poor Testimony of Tourists and Other Non-Locals Who Are Assumed to be Christians.

Common Spiritual, Cultural/Social and Other Bridges to the Gospel

1. Dreams and Visions About Jesus (or someone coming with an important message).
2. Brokenness:
   - Physical: Due to war, drought, famine, disease, handicaps, and birth defects.
   - Social: Imprisonment, corporal punishment, social stigma, occupation, and self-abasement because of rank or caste.
   - Spiritual: Due to special work of the Holy Spirit (Paul's experience).
3. Testimonies or Examples From Peers or Other Respected Persons.
4. Commonality in Heritage Stories — Heroes, Deliverers, Worthy Persons, and Famous Leaders.
5. Cultural Stories That Parallel Bible Stories.
6. Local Proverbs, Expressions Like Four-Character Sayings in Chinese, and Etymology of Words (Biblical meaning roots in Chinese characters).
7. Social and Cultural Practices in Bible Stories That are Like or in Agreement With the Local Social Norms and Culture.
8. Desire for Relief From Fear, Danger, or Other Oppressive Causes (whether real or imagined).
9. Desire for Physical Needs Being Met: Housing, clothing, food, water, and medicine.
10. Desire for a Higher Moral or Spiritual Way: Search for peace, social stability, and ethical concerns.
11. Desire for Literacy, English as Second Language, or Education.
12. Desire for Honor, Social Recognition, Meaning of Life.

13. Desire for Relationship and Fellowship to Overcome Loneliness or Alienation.
14. Exposure to Persistent, Pervasive, Culturally Apprpriate Media Messages: Radio, TV, and/or print correspondence courses.
15. Curiosity About What the Bible Teaches, Desire to Learn From the Bible.
16. Prior Knowledge About God, Jesus, or Christianity: Due to present religion or contact with Christians.
17. Signs & Wonders, Healing (knowing the Jesus of healing or deliverance from evil spirits).
18. A "Failed" Religion: In need or distress the present religion failed to provide help.
19. Interest to Fill in Knowledge Gaps About the Spirit World and the Real World.
20. Genealogical Interest & Concerns About Families and Ancestors.
21. Similarities in Religious Vocabulary That are in Agreement With the Bible and Christianity.
22. Bible Stories With Plots or Outcomes That are in Agreement With or Similar to Local Worldview.
23. Teaching Methodology That is Sensitive to Listeners' Learning Preferences Whether Oral or Literate.
24. Teaching Methodology That is Well Organized for Target Audience and Paced for Comfortable Learning.
25. Teaching in Correct Designated Places for Truth, by Acceptable Teachers and at Acceptable Times.
26. Use of Heart Language of the People for Teaching.
27. Teaching at a Time When People are not Preoccupied With Their Agriculture or Other Work.
28. Teaching at a Time When are no Disruptive Festivals That Distract People and Preoccupy Their Time and Interest.
29. Providing Appropriate Teaching Content Selected and Organized for Listeners if Needs by Sex, Age, or Social

Status are Different.

30. Embedding the Storying Event in a "Community Time" When Time is Used for Fellowship and Relationship Building.

31. Awareness of Redemptive Analogies Among a People: Examples of where God is already at work preparing a people to hear the Gospel and providing redemptive illustrations — words, present and historical events, dreams and other signs that point to salvation but are not redemptive in themselves.

Short-Dialog Question Lists for Non-literate Storyers

Bangladesh Dialog Questions

1. What happened in the story? (*Basic plot or storyline*)
2. What did God say or do? (*Did God warn, promise, or give a command?*)
3. What did the people say or do? (*Did the people listen, respond, and obey?*)
4. How did the story turn out? Good or bad? (The outcome)
5. What did you learn from the story? (*New truths or something meaningful to you*)
6. Now that you have heard the story, what should you do? (How am I going to apply what I have learned?)[75]

Ethiopia Dialog Questions

1. What part of the story do you like the best?
2. What part of the story is hard to hear or troubles you?
3. What parts of the story are hard to understand or do you have questions about?
4. What does the story say about God?
5. What part of the story would you like to tell someone else or reflect on yourself? Why?

Expanded Discovery Questions

1. What do you like best about the story? (*key question*)
    - *What do you find encouraging? (expanded or interpretive questions)*
    - *What is the most helpful?*
    - *What do you get excited about in this story (reading, poem, etc.)?*
    - *What are the most important issues?*
    - *What is the best part of this story for you?*
    - *What does this help explain?*
2. What do you like least about the story? (*I normally do not like negative questions, but you may get helpful information from this—jot.*)
    - *What is disturbing?*
    - *What is surprising or hard to hear?*
    - *What kind of problems does this present for you?*
    - *Is there anything that makes you uncomfortable?*
    - *What do you wish were left out of the story?*
    - *What is most difficult for you?*
3. What do you not understand in the story?
    - *What do you wish you had an answer for?*
    - *What questions in your mind does the story raise?*
    - *Discuss anything that you find confusing.*
    - *What questions do you have?*
    - *Is there anything that you find confusing?*
    - *Is there anything you would like to know more about?*
    - *Which parts of the story puzzle you?*
    - *What parts of the story are difficult to understand?*
    - *Is there anything you would like to learn more about?*

4. What do you learn about God from the story?
   - *What kinds of things can we know for certain?*
   - *How is God different from man?*
   - *How does this change or illuminate your picture of God?*
   - *What do you wish you had known before?*
   - *What impression of God do you get from this reading (story)?*
   - *How would you describe God?*
5. What do you personally need to do about it?
   - *What is one thing you need to change?*
   - *What do you find immediately helpful?*
   - *If this (story) is true, what should you do?*
   - *What relationship is there between what you have read (or heard) and your own life?*
   - *Is there any truth here to which you want to respond?*
   - *What do you want to say to God?*
   - *What do you want to build into your life?*
6. Which phrase or verse from the story do you want to take with you and think about this week?
   - *Which phrase or verse will help you this week?*
   - *What nugget of truth will you take with you?*
   - *Is there anything you want to share with someone else this week?*
   - *To which part of this story will you cling?*
   - *What do you most want to remember?*
   - *Which promise would you like to remember in times of need?*
   - *Which part of this reading (or story) do you want to become a part of your thinking?*[76]

(These lists are resources to assist forming your own discussion dialog. Select the ones that best help your listeners to interact with the stories. The object in the short list is to establish a list of exploratory questions that can be readily remembered and used over and over by local storyers who may be oral communicators, not able to read from a written lesson or follow a written discussion guide.)

The International Orality Network (ION)

The International Orality Network connects people who are reaching oral communicators as well as unreached people groups (UPGs) to storying and storytelling resources and training.

Vision: To influence the body of Christ to make disciples of all oral learners.

Mission: The International Orality Network which is made up of "Great Commission" ministries, missionaries and local churches who seek to:

- *Raise awareness of the difference between orality and literacy among agencies, churches and individuals engaged in great commission ministry*
- *Cast vision for launching indigenously led CPMs among unreached oral cultures*
- *Provide consultations and training for those seeking to be more effective in making disciples of oral preference learners*
- *Influence great commission gatekeepers and thought leaders internationally to focus more on reaching oral learners and utilizing appropriate strategies and best practices*
- *Provide consultations and training for those seeking to be more effective in making disciples of secondary orality learners*
- *Serve as a clearing house for research and best practices for discipling oral learners and secondary orality learners.*
- *For more information see: http://ion2008.niny.com*

Chapter 23
REFERENCES

---

[1] William Morris, ed., *American Heritage Dictionary of the English Language* (New York, NY: Houghton Mifflin Company, 1969).

[2] Hans Rudi Weber, *The Communication of the Gospel to Illiterates* (London: SCM Press Ltd., 1957) 18.

[3] Johannes G. Warneck, *The Living Christ and Dying Heathenism* (Grand Rapids, MI: Baker Book House, 1954) 224, 225.

[4] Walter J. Ong, *Orality and Literacy: the Technologizing of the Word* (London and New York: Routledge, 1982).

[5] Dell G. and Rachel Sue Schultze, *God and Man* (Manila, PHILIPPINES: Church Strengthening Ministry, 1984).

[6] David (Dubby) Rodda, "Sharing the Gospel With Muslims: A Chronological Approach," *SEEDBED* (West Sussex, UK: Arab World Ministries, vol VII, no. 4, 1992).

[7] Jacob A. Loewen, *Culture and Human Values: Christian Intervention in Anthropological Perspective* (Pasadena, CA: Wm. Carey Library, 1975) 374.

[8] Schultze 1984.

[9] Rodda 1992.

[10] CESA Kanga Storying Cloth, http://imbresources.org/index.cfm/fa/store.prod/ProdID/1619.cfm

[11] LaNette W. Thompson, *What Jesus Wants His Disciples to Know and Do* (COTE D'IVOIRE: International Mission Board, SBC, 1999).

[12] Fritz Sprunger, compiling editor, *The Gospel Encounters the Japanese Worldview* (Tokyo, JAPAN: Hayama Missionary Seminar, 28th Annual Report, 1987).

[13] Tim Castagna, Paul Burnham, and Peter Baker, *The Ibaloi Barriers* (Manila, PHILIPPINES: New Tribes Mission unpublished paper, 1988).

[14] *"Ee-taow!"* (Sanford, FL: New Tribes Mission, video account of evangelizing the Mouk people via Chronological Bible Teaching, 1989).

[15] Genesis 25:34, NIV.

---

[16] Richard L. Pratt, Jr., *He Gave Us Stories: The Bible Student's Guide to Interpreting Old Testament Narratives* (Phillipsburg, PA: Presbyterian and Reformed Publishing Company, 1990).

[17] Thomas E. Boomershine, *Story Journey: An Invitation to the Gospel as Storytelling* (Nashville, TN: Abingdon Press, 1988).

[18] George Walker and Bob Kennell, *Evangelizing Cross-Culturally: The Bisorio Example* (Sanford, FL: New Tribes Mission Research & Planning Department, 1989).

[19] Bryan and Diane Thomas as translated from original Cebuano by Jeff and Regina Palmer, *Chronological Storytelling (54 Bible Stories),* (Manila, PHILIPPINES: Church Strengthening Ministry, 1991).

[20] Kristen Hoatson, (in Africa) unpublished report by Peggy Rose.

[21] Martin Goldsmith, as quoted by Bill A. Musk, *Touching the Soul of Islam* (Monrovia, CA: MARC, 1995).

[22] David Rodda, *"Sharing the Gospel With Muslims: A Chronological Approach," SEEDBED* (West Sussex, UK: Arab World Ministry, Vol. VII, no. 4).

[23] *"Ee-taow!"* (New Tribes Mission, 1991).

[24] Bryan and Diane Thomas (1991).

[25] Schultze, (1984).

[26] John D. Wilson, *"What It Takes To Reach People in Oral Cultures"* (Evangelical Missions Quarterly, vol. 27, no. 2, April, 1991) 154-158.

[27] Aleksandr Romanovich Luria, *Cognitive Development: Its Cultural and Social Foundations*, ed. Michael Cole, trans. By Martin Lopez-Morillas and Lynn Solotaroff (Cambridge, MA and London: Harvard University Press, 1976) 108, 114.

[28] LaNette W. Thompson, "*Diaradugu Diary*" (International Mission Board, SBC, unpublished report, May, 1991).

[29] Thompson, "*Diary,*" 1991.

[30] Thompson, "*Diary,*" 1991, p 3.

[31] "Ee-taow!," New Tribes Mission (1991).

[32] Schultze, (3-4).

[33] Thompson, *(*1991) 3.

[34] J. O. Terry, *The Suffering Servant* (SINGAPORE: International Mission Board, SBC, 2000).

[35] "*Ee-taow*!," New Tribes Mission (1991).

[36] *JESUS Film*, Campus Crusade International.

[37] Jacob A. Loewen, *Bible Stories: Message and Matrix: Culture and Human Values* (South Pasadena, CA: William Carey Library) 375.

[38] Thompson, "*Diary*," 9, 10.

[39] Thompson, "*Diary*," 10, 11.

[40] Caloy Gabuco, "*Telling the Story...*" (Manila, PHILIPPINES: Church Strengthening Ministry and Sanford, FL: New Tribes Mission Bookroom, 1983).

[41] bookstore_hq@ntm.org.

[42] Johani Gauran, *The Witnessing Kit* (Manila, PHILIPPINES: Church Strengthening Ministry, 1991).

[43] Betty Lukens, "*Through the Bible in Felt*," 1966.

[44] *Vie de Jesus MAFA*, 24, rue du Maréchal-Joffre, 78000 Versailles, FRANCE (look in local Catholic bookstores in Africa).

[45] MegaVoice, www.megavoice.com .

[46] Proclaimer, www.faithcomesbyhearing.com

[47] Avery T. Willis, Jr., "*Following Jesus: Making Disciples of Oral Learners*" (Laguna Hills, CA: Progressive Vision, 2003).

[48] J.O.Terry, *Hope Stories* from the Bible (Fort Worth, TX, 2004).

[49] J.O.Terry, "*God's Gift: Forgiveness of Sin and Peace For Women*" (Fort Worth, TX, unpublished story set, 2004).

[50] Roy W. Fairchild, *LIFESTORY CONVERSATIONS* (New York, NY: Evangelism Program of the United Presbyterian Church, USA, 1977).

[51] George and May Ingram, *24 Bible Stories for Village Workers* (Calcutta, INDIA: Evangelical Literature Depot).

[52] Gauran, (1991).

[53] Jeff & Regina Palmer, *Chronological Storytelling: Telling the Bible Story* (Manila, PHILIPPINES: Church Strengthening Ministry, 1991).

[54] Loewen, (1984).

[55] Christy Brawner, "*Good News of Jesus*" Evangelistic lessons, (Brazil: brawner@pobox.com).

[56] Blair Faulk, "*The Storying Scarf*" (www.storyingscarf.com).

[57] J.O.Terry, "*Water Stories from the Bible,*" (Fort Worth, TX: rev. 2003).

[58] J.O.Terry, "*Hope Stories from the Bible*" (Fort Worth, TX: 2004).

[59] Gary and Evelyn Harthcock, www.centralbaptist.net/page33.html

[60] chronologicalbiblestorying.com/esl_efl/esl_efl_tips.htm

[61] Kevin Greeson, *Camel Training Manual* (INDIA: WIGTAKE Resources 2004).

[62] OneStory, www.onestory.org/Partners.

[63] Terry, *Water Stories from the Bible.*

[64] Gauran, (1991).

[65] Faulk, "*Storying Scarf.*"

[66] www.wsaresourcesite.org/Topics/storying.htm

[67] www.centralbaptist.net/page33.html

[68] Terry, *Hope Stories from the Bible.*

[69] J.O.Terry, *Short-Term Mission Manual* (SINGAPORE: International Mission Board, SBC, 1999).

[70] Fairchild (1977).

[71] resources.imb.org/index.cfm/fa/store.prod/ProdID/1218.cfm.

[72] Biblestorying@sbcglobal.net for reference materials.

[73] Carla, Clements, www.VisualStoryBible.org.

[74] J.O.Terry, "Bible Storying" quarterly newsletter for Bible storyers, biblestorying@sbcglobal.net.

[75] As shared in the agricultural and Bible training program, Development Service Center, Savar, BANGLADESH.

[76] Adapted from list shared by Tammy Lundquist.